C000097046

THE URBAN

BLOCK

A GUIDE FOR URBAN DESIGNERS, ARCHITECTS AND TOWN PLANNERS

JONATHAN TARBATT & CHLOE STREET TARBATT

RIBA Publishing

© RIBA Publishing, 2020

Published by RIBA Publishing, 66 Portland Place, London, W1B 1AD

ISBN 978 1 85946 874 6

The rights of Jonathan Tarbatt and Chloe Street Tarbatt to be identified as the Authors of this Work have been asserted in accordance with the Copyright, Designs and Patents Act 1988 sections 77 and 78.

British Library Cataloguing-in-Publication Data

A catalogue record for this book is available from the British Library.

Commissioning Editor: Alex White
Assistant Editor: Clare Holloway
Production: Sarah-Louise Deazley
Designed and typeset by Sarah-Louise Deazley
Printed and bound by L.E.G.O. spa

While every effort has been made to check the accuracy and quality of the information given in this publication, neither the Authors nor the Publisher accept any responsibility for the subsequent use of this information, for any errors or omissions that it may contain, or for any misunderstandings arising from it.

www.ribapublishing.com

CONTENTS

ACKNOWLEDGEMENTS

We are very grateful to the architectural practices who so generously contributed drawings and photographs of their work, as well as others who helped by supplying maps or other information. We also benefitted from a Faculty Teaching Award bestowed on Chloe by the University of Kent, which went some way towards meeting the costs of travel and photography.

We are also very grateful for the unstinting support and generosity of our parents: Jon's parents, David and Ruth Tarbatt, and Chloe's mum, Joanna Lowry, who also looked after our young children, Thomas and Hugo, while we were struggling to finish the book. We're sure Chloe's father, the late Professor Brian Street, would be proud, and would be the first to propose a toast! Last (but not least), many thanks to the RIBA team, especially commissioning editor Alex White for taking us on, assistant editor Clare Holloway for keeping us on track, and production and design assistant Sarah-Louise Deazley, for making us look good.

ABOUT THE AUTHORS

Jonathan Tarbatt, BA, BSc, BArch, MRUP, MA (Urban Design), RTPI, RIBA

Jonathan is an Urban Designer, Chartered Architect and Town Planner with over 25 years' experience in the public and private sectors in the UK, Australia and Ireland. The depth and breadth of his experience and education in these three disciplines, together with his academic background in urban geography and sociology, has given him a multidisciplinary perspective and a unique level of expertise in the built environment. He is the author of *The Plot – Designing Diversity in the Built Environment*, and has also contributed to a range of books and industry journals, focusing on the impact of urban form on environmental quality. He is an active practitioner and combines his consultancy work with teaching at the Kent School of Architecture and Planning (KSAP).

Chloe Street Tarbatt, BSc, MArch (RCA), ARB, PGCHE

Chloe is an architect and a lecturer at the Kent School of Architecture and Planning (KSAP). Following 10 years' practice experience working on a range of high-profile, award-winning cultural and educational projects with Dixon Jones (London) and de Blacam and Meagher Architects (Dublin), she taught at the University for the Creative Arts before joining KSAP, where she is currently the BA Programme Director for Architecture. Her research interests include the psychology of urban experience, architectural representation and pedagogy. Chloe continues to combine private practice with teaching.

A NOTE ON ILLUSTRATIVE BLOCK DIAGRAMS

The block plans we have produced to illustrate the history of the block and our case examples have been redrawn from a variety of different sources, including open-source mapping, national mapping agencies and architects' own plans and drawings. We have supplemented these sources with information from aerial photography and site visits, where relevant. All of the block diagrams are oriented to north, and so north points have not been added to the plans.

To allow the reader to compare and contrast the examples, we have (with one or two exceptions) reproduced the plans to the same scale, regardless of the size of the block. Given the widely varying level of detail available for each project, this has meant adding detail in some cases (e.g. from aerial photography) and stripping it back in others. In doing so it became apparent in some cases that there were minor discrepancies between the detail we were provided with, and what has been built. Of course, buildings change, and designs can be altered during construction. This is especially the case regarding historical examples, where a great deal of time has passed since their original conception and the availability of mapping to us. In regard to the contemporary case examples, we have tried to pick up some of these discrepancies along the way to make them more accurate, however we cannot claim they are accurate in the fullest sense. Having said that, of course, we would argue that the examples have been chosen for more significant reasons than can be undermined by such small details, and we hope that this comes across clearly in what follows.

INTRODUCTION

This book is about the block. It focuses on a kind of urban block known to designers and urban morphologists as the 'perimeter block': a type that has dominated urban (and suburban) development for millennia. The perimeter block has a long but chequered history: it has fallen in and out of favour over time for a variety of reasons. Its pure form is most commonly found in cities, but it has been adapted to suburban development, albeit with mixed results. Today, it is promoted by academics and 'best practice' guidelines as the outstanding kind of block that masterplanners and urban designers can deploy to create successful streets and spaces. But there are many and varied forms the perimeter block can take, each with its own strengths and weaknesses, and the perimeter block itself is neither a reliable indicator of urban quality nor is it appropriate to every urban or suburban condition.

ABOUT THE BOOK

Much has been written about urban form that directly or indirectly touches on the block, but there is very little that brings together the myriad considerations that go into block design and layout in one place. Our aim is to fill this gap in a coherent way.

Chapter 1 sets out our understanding of the block. It includes a brief discussion of prominent theorists and how their ideas have infiltrated into contemporary notions of 'best practice', and their concurrent implications for urban design. A basic knowledge of the history and theory of the block is necessary to understand and read urban form today. As urban designers and architects, we combine our awareness of urban context with direct observation to engender some reflection on the scale of urban form that mediates between the city and individual buildings. It demonstrates a useful point that there is no one way to build a city or suburb.

Chapter 2 develops a simple taxonomy of urban forms, including the main block types. This helps to define the basic block types that are in common use, and hints at variants or hybrid forms that have emerged, or might yet emerge. The main features of each type are outlined, with the implications for each on urban life.

These 'implications' lie at the core of the book, because they raise questions about how urban designers and architects should set about designing blocks to create convivial places with high-quality streets and spaces. The issues designers must grapple with range from lofty ideals related to equality of access versus exclusivity of access, down to how and where to park cars and store rubbish bins. Somewhere in between, the way in which buildings interface between the public and private realms must also be designed, and this raises yet more questions: What is the nature of the transitional space between the back of the public footpath and the building threshold? What uses, entrances or activities will be encouraged to 'face' the street, if any? To what extent will movement through the block be regulated?

These are just some of the questions posed in Chapter 3, and some forms of block design are better at answering them than others. Subsequently, we'll examine the syntactic relationships between buildings and streets that block designers must consider. At this point – the dialectical relationship between the block and the street – we must acknowledge that our study is underpinned by Western assumptions. Consequently, we spend less time looking at urban forms where buildings intentionally 'turn away' from the street than those that actively address it. Where we include traditional Arabic urban forms, we do so primarily to illustrate the essential difference in their treatment of the public and private realms, while recognising that in any case new urban development in many Arabic cities often adopts 'Western' models anyway.

We explore these issues further in Chapter 4, with reference to case examples. The case examples are drawn from a variety of places and contexts, both 'urban' and 'suburban'. Low-density suburban forms are often criticised for being wasteful of land and resources,[1] but we feel that it is important and valid to study these suburban forms, if only because they are a fact of life.

Developers and house-builders – those holding the purse strings, so to speak – have their own agendas, however, and they often prefer different forms. We look at other kinds of block too, and how the perimeter block has been adapted and changed to suit different circumstances and conditions. There are also circumstances where a variety of different approaches can, and have, been used successfully in the past. We hope that through examining the perimeter block and its close cousins, we can demonstrate its continued relevance to placemaking, whether suburban or urban, while recognising that a dogmatic approach is not necessarily the best way forward.

WHY THE (PERIMETER) BLOCK

Without the block, there would be no streets, just roads. Without streets, there would be no street life, just traffic. Without street life, there would be no city, just buildings. In more prosaic terms, the block is no more than the land and building area defined by streets. But it is the nature of the interface between the two that has a critical impact on the quality of the spaces between those buildings.

To understand why this is true, it is necessary to appreciate that the city is more than the sum of its individual buildings. It is made up of built elements – urban blocks – that mediate between the scale of individual buildings and the scale of wider neighbourhoods or quarters. By extension, these elements also mediate between the private domain of the individual, and the public realm. As such, they have been called 'the building blocks of the city'.[2]

The importance of the block to city life is well rehearsed, and in any case, we seldom find ourselves in the business of making cities from scratch.[3] But we are in the business of making new houses, neighbourhoods and new local centres, and we need lots of them: 250,000 a year to be imprecise.[4]

UNDERSTANDING THE BLOCK

Understanding the history of urban form, and particularly the urban block, is essential to understanding the urban context within which we are designing today. Without an understanding of what works and why, we cannot hope to exert a positive influence on the urban fabric. Following this premise, this chapter outlines a short history of urban form, explaining how certain historical processes have affected patterns of urban development and consequently, the formation of urban blocks.

THE BLOCK, THE PLOT AND THE STREET

The traditional urban block cannot be understood as a discrete entity. Rather it is one element of a system that depends both on its symbiotic relationship to the street and on the substrate of subdivisions that divide it into smaller, more or less independent units of land holding known as plots or lots. In turn, these plots can be occupied by different buildings and potentially have different uses or combinations of uses. This underlying structure implies a 'built in' capacity for change, for which the plot is the underlying framework. As Panerai et al. put it: 'To think of the block as a whole would be missing the point, and reducing it to a continuous and homogeneous built up area surrounding an empty centre...risks showing the outward appearance of urbanity without ensuring the conditions that allow it to happen.'[1] Put simply, the fabric of older towns and cities has evolved through this superimposition of several structures operating at different scales to produce different yet coherent urban forms.

This historic practice, to masterplan by plot and block together, where the owner of every plot is left to their own devices, has been superseded in the modern era by a tendency to masterplan by block alone, where the block is produced by the space left over after the street has been defined, and each block or series of blocks is developed by a single entity (the developers). Contemporary masterplanning practice tends to reduce the block to a single 'super plot' to be occupied by a single building (or sometimes a group of buildings which are nonetheless 'joined at the hip' by means of a shared basement or podium). In this new normal, the plot is no longer part of the development equation, and so an invisible yet fundamental structuring element of the 'old town' has been removed. Once this is understood, we can begin to understand why historic blocks have managed to evolve and change to meet new conditions, and why modern blocks are more likely to be replaced in their entirety when they are no longer fit for purpose.

1.1 Aerial view of the Roman City of Timgad,[2] Algeria, dating to the 1st century BCE. The blocks, or 'insulae', measure approximately 21m².

THE BLOCK IN ANTIQUITY

This potted history begins around the turn of the common era (CE) at the outset of the Roman Empire, during which the significant term 'insula' (plural 'insulae'), meaning 'island', was coined to denote both an apartment building and an urban block. The term 'island' is instructive because the block takes its form from the streets that surround it. In other words, it is the area of private land surrounded by public streets. Gates[3] estimates that 90% of the population of Ancient Rome lived in insulae, and as such, they constituted the general fabric of the city, punctuated by shops, public buildings and more salubrious villas. To form an 'island' requires more than one street. This essentially differentiates the block, which sits within a network of streets, from the linear nature of streets on their own: the street must change direction more than once for a block to be formed. Second, one 'island' on its own does not a city make.

The Ancient Greeks are credited with the rational masterplanning of new cities in orthogonal grid patterns at least four centuries earlier than this, during the late classical period of the 5th and 4th centuries BCE (e.g. Miletus, Piraeus, Olynthos and Priene). Describing excavated Greek houses at ancient Olynthos, for example, Gates[4] states: 'Blocks of adjacent houses sharing walls are neatly arranged along straight streets, laid out in parallel lines. Houses are similarly hidden from the street by an enclosure wall, and inside, the courtyard is the focus.'[5] Parallel to the gridded masterplans taking place in classical Greece, such layouts were emerging elsewhere, with similar examples found in Babylon (present-day Iraq).

This gridded approach developed by the Ancient Greeks and other early civilisations was highly influential on Roman city planners (e.g. Timgad, North Africa; see Figure 1.1), who continued the practice as part of a ritualistic process, culminating in the distribution of building plots by lottery.[6] Although Timgad seems a somewhat random case – isolated as it is in the barren landscape of North Africa – its function as a garrison town is very much representative of a formula that was established for new fort towns across Africa, Gaul and Britain during the Roman Empire, and illustrates the far-reaching and long-lasting effects of classically inspired Roman town planning.

There are two relevant points that arise from these early examples of gridded masterplanning. Firstly, that the practice of creating a masterplan that defines urban blocks has a long history, and secondly, that these blocks were (at least initially) occupied by internally oriented courtyard houses, and as such did not address the streets that they enclosed.

This relationship to the street appears to have been fundamentally altered by later Roman city building. Urban remains at the mercantile Roman city of Ostia have been relatively well preserved and the archaeological excavations of four-storey insulae dating to the 3rd century BCE[7] show an urban form we can more readily associate with contemporary urban blocks (see Figure 1.2). The excavated block at Ostia is lined with shops at street level, with a series of passages and entrances leading to apartments overlooking the public street and a garden courtyard. The interior of the block contains shared open space with two further apartment blocks, and as such, creates what we define as a 'nested perimeter block'.

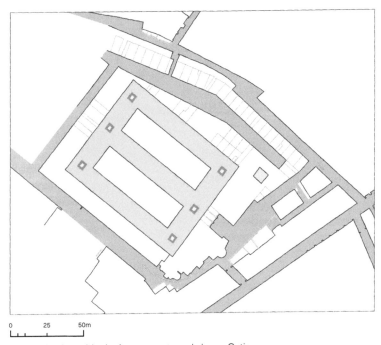

0   25   50m

1.2 A mixed-use block of apartments and shops, Ostia.

THE MEDIEVAL BLOCK

A new phase of urban development took place during the medieval period, between the 10th and 11th centuries CE, during which the political and economic climate in Europe regained some semblance of stability. The direct corollary of the masterplanned city of the Greeks and Romans (whether gridded or adopting a radial or other pattern) is the unplanned, seemingly 'organic' one, which is most commonly associated with the medieval towns developed during this period. As Spiro Kostof[8] argues in *The City Shaped: Urban Patterns* and *Meanings Through History*, this apparent dichotomy is problematic. What reads as unordered may on closer examination prove to be an 'irregular pattern'. Rather than being 'unplanned', it is more accurate to suggest that such forms resulted from the accumulated decisions of a greater number of agents over a longer period of time. It is also well documented that 'new' medieval towns (i.e. ones that did not inherit a pre-existing urban form) were often laid out by surveyors, albeit on occasion not very accurate ones.[9] Because medieval land division was fixed with reference to metes and bounds (natural features or pre-urban land divisions and pathways), as well as with the use of instruments, it is not surprising that the results would yield seemingly organic forms, which contrast with the more orderly gridded masterplans of both earlier and subsequent eras.

Understanding the historical forces that brought these organic-seeming urban forms into being helps to explain the diversity of block formation that emerged during this medieval period.

According to Hindle[10] there are five types of medieval plan layouts found in Britain:

- Towns with central marketplaces (usually triangular owing to the meeting of three roads).
- Linear towns (usually a street with a widening to accommodate a marketplace).
- Castle towns (often consisting of a single street running from the castle gates and surrounded by a protective ditch or wall).
- Rectilinear plans (planned towns with a rectilinear block pattern, extending to a few examples with gridded plans consisting of more than twelve rectilinear blocks).
- Composite plans (plans that grew in different ways over time, for example organic in origin with planned extensions or alternatively planned cores with ad hoc extensions).

Elsewhere, in the later medieval period, bastide towns – established in Southern France, Northern Spain, the Netherlands and Wales – took on a more deliberately gridded arrangement. The more orderly form of these settlements can be read as an expression of control by wealthy nobles over land for farming, trade and defence over contested territories.[11]

Together these illustrate the complexity of urban morphology as an area of study, serving to highlight some of the factors that challenge the conventional assumption that the block is either the result of a rational masterplan (i.e. gridded) or the result of happenstance (i.e. organic). Rather the history of urban form is multi-layered, with places being subject to multiple influences over time. Where a block layout originally formed as the result of a gridded masterplan, this order may also be disrupted by later occupiers. For example, the Roman grid is outward-related but the Islamic 'block' is inward-looking, and so Roman gridded towns that were taken over by Muslim invaders were re-moulded to suit the cultural and religious norms of Islam. Different processes disrupted the grid in the West, for example the primacy of the marketplace was asserted over and above the Roman forum and asserted a radial hierarchy of movement for which the grid is not so well suited.[12]

One such city is London. Within the Roman city walls the primary streets maintained their original alignments but over time the grid was disrupted and made more irregular. In Figure 1.3 the medieval block is at first subdivided into generous burgage plots occupied by street buildings, with space for cooking, workshops and market gardening within the interior of the block.[13] As the population grows and demand for space within the walls intensifies, there is a pattern of further subdivision of the plots, together with gradual encroachment of buildings inwards. In some cases, the original plots are infilled completely with a sub-set of single-aspect dwellings accessed by a narrow court.

Changes to the economic structure of towns in the 19th and early 20th centuries saw a gradual reversal of subdivisions, leading to an amalgamation of plots to suit new building types. The earliest available Ordnance Survey mapping of the medieval city of Canterbury (which was also founded atop a Roman settlement), shows how the grain of plots that make up the block are gradually increased in size over the period of a century (see Figure 1.4). The left-hand block shows the former Buttermarket at the upper north-western side, adjacent to the Cathedral Precincts. The Buttermarket is typical of many medieval towns, as it was formed at the intersection of three radial routes, with direct access to the Cathedral Precincts. Following bomb damage sustained during World War II the redevelopment reinstated the former medieval lane known as Longmarket, dividing the 19th century block back into two separate blocks. The plan introduced a new open space on the south-eastern side and was designed in a historicist manner to recreate the appearance of individual buildings occupying small plots. Although the appearance is deemed satisfactory insofar as it 'fits in' with its authentically historic surroundings,[14] it is important to note that the block cannot function in quite the same way as its medieval neighbour, because the buildings are not independent of one another. The interior of the block is raised on a podium accessed from the street and as such is shared by the buildings surrounding it. Although the rear configuration is fundamentally altered, the outward facing units share the pre-eminent relationship between the block and the street that is characteristic of many medieval towns.

1.3 (Left) Medieval block, London (note the pattern of plot subdivision within the block, if any, is not known). (Right) The same block mapped in 1677 by John Ogilby and William Morgan, showing the dense pattern of plot subdivision, leading in some cases to the development of 'court' housing in what would have started its urban life as a single plot.

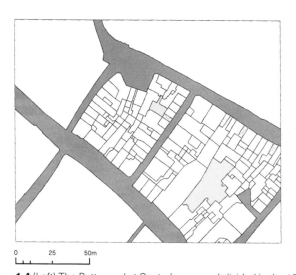
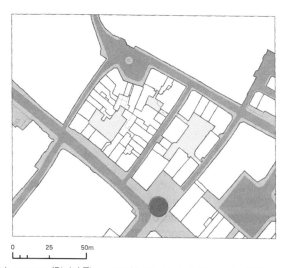

1.4 (Left) The Buttermarket Canterbury, as subdivided in the 19th century. (Right) The same block as subdivided in the 20th century.

NEOCLASSICAL AND BAROQUE BLOCK PATTERNS

Prior to the 19th century the accumulated wealth of the British Empire, derived from its colonies, facilitated new masterplanned extensions to several major cities. The Georgian terrace (a form of row house) reinvented the medieval townhouse in the classical manner and recombined it with masterplanned extensions following classical principles. The results, for example Edinburgh New Town, Bath, the Gardiner and Fitzwilliam Estates in Dublin and Belgravia in London, were formed essentially of mews blocks, hierarchically separating the main residence (fronting the street) from the buildings serving it (accessed from a rear lane called a mews), and thereby avoiding the need for its wealthy inhabitants to mix with the hoi polloi. As the mews block lends itself to orthogonal forms, the so-called 'great estates' were largely gridded, albeit with the inclusion of set-piece architectural compositions characteristic of the period such as crescents and circuses, and by formal squares and gardens.

With the growth of the middle classes the mews block was recast in simpler form as the row block, with simple houses backing onto one another or sharing a rear access lane. This, in a variety of price brackets, formed the staple of suburbanisation in Britain throughout the Victorian era (mid to late 19th century) through to the Edwardian period and well into the 20th century. Growing concern over the deprivations of overcrowding and poverty led in the UK to the adoption of certain by-laws imposing minimum standards on the block. So-called 'by-law housing', adopted locally from 1840 and nationally by 1877,[15] represented a step up from medieval courts with better sanitation, lighting, separation of living functions and higher ceilings, etc. Row blocks with a rear access lane also facilitated the collection of foul waste from outdoor privies.

The newly laid out suburbs of row housing lent themselves to long blocks laid out in grids but, as illustrated in Figure 1.5, these were generally unrelieved by open space, parks or gardens.

In comparison, Baroque planning favoured the dynamism of the diagonal and the circus over the grid, and although not wholeheartedly adopted by the English, this radically altered the shape of Paris and numerous absolutist states (see Figure 1.6).

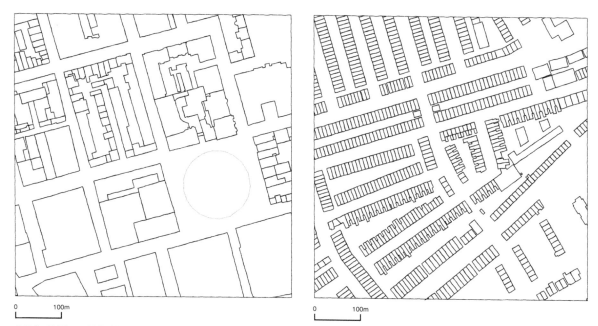

1.5 (Left) The gridded blocks of Georgian Belgravia punctuated by formal squares. (Right) Victorian terraced housing from the 19th century.

1.6 (Left) Paris after re-planning by Hausmann in the Baroque manner. (Right) The Parisian Left Bank – one of the few areas of Paris unaffected by Hausmann.

BLOCK PLANNING IN THE NEW WORLD

Where the grid lost out to the diagonal in some places (e.g. Washington), it was adopted in swathes across both North and South America, where with a few exceptions (e.g. New Haven) it became the default model for colonialization from the early 16th century in South America through to the late 18th century in North America.

One of the most well-known gridiron plans, Manhattan, typifies this approach (see Figure 1.7). The Common Council of New York appointed Commissioners at the beginning of the 19th century to lay out a plan for Manhattan (known as 'the Commissioner's Plan'), which they duly produced in 1811, based on a repeating grid of rectangular blocks. At first glance Manhattan's grid appears relentless, but while the width of every block is the same, the length of blocks varies. Its grid embodies a hierarchy of movement related to the wider avenues and narrower cross streets. The diagonal of Broadway relieves the monotony by cutting across the grid, although like Cerdà's Barcelona, the lone diagonal seems to be an afterthought. But whereas the grid for Manhattan is largely uninterrupted by parks or open spaces, there are other, more sophisticated precedents worthy of closer inspection.

Savannah, Georgia, regarded by Campbell[16] as a masterpiece of planned urbanism, is a relatively early example (see Figure 1.8). Rather than simply repeating near identical blocks, the Savannah grid is made up of a sequence of discrete but repeating block modules – superblocks – each imbued with its own hierarchy of movement, form, function and open space.

Laid out in 1733, each 'superblock' comprised a 'ward' with a square at the centre. The western and eastern sides of the square were flanked with plots reserved for civic and commercial buildings. The northern and southern sides were reserved for houses. According to Kostof,[17] the ward was made up of four tithings, each composed of ten freeholders with a constable at the head. The 40 house plots in each ward were arranged as row blocks with a shared alley or service lane. Because the house plots lined east–west streets, the wards were united visually, and, of course, houses lining the edge of one ward faced the houses lining the edge of the neighbouring ward as well. The first wards became the centre of the growing town, but the module was used for later expansion well into the 19th century. Beyond that, the surviving wards are no longer composed of tithings, and most of the central blocks have undergone a process of plot amalgamation to facilitate the kinds of larger-scale buildings and uses associated with the modern city (see Figure 1.9). Nevertheless, the hierarchy of block structure has proved itself to be immensely successful and adaptable to change, incorporating intimate pedestrian streets with cafés and restaurants and public parks, surrounded by larger-scale civic and employment uses (see Figure 1.10).

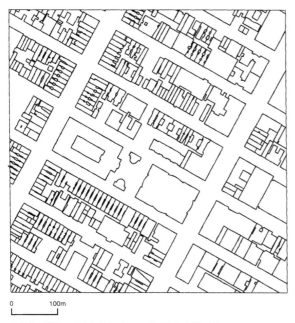

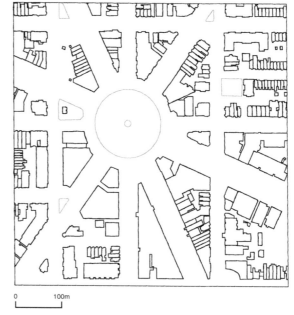

1.7 (Left) New York (Manhattan). (Right) Washington.

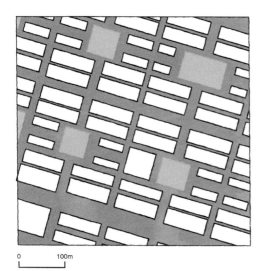

1.8 Savannah ward blocks showing the superblock structure, with smaller blocks nested within a movement hierarchy.

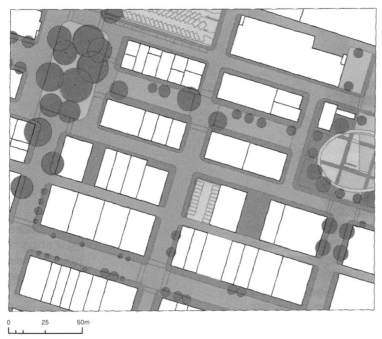

0　25　50m

1.9 Mixed-use blocks within a ward in Savannah.

1.10 View of pedestrian street in Savannah accessing the mixed-use blocks.

GRIDIRON BLOCKS IN EUROPE

Barcelona was extended in line with an 1858 plan by Cerdà, again using the tried and trusted gridiron plan, but this time with chamfered square blocks of around 113m. Although Cerdà's plan was bisected by a diagonal 'X', this almost seems an afterthought compared to Hausmann's Parisian adventure. The contrast in form between the 'old city', with its pre-existing medieval form, and its 'planned' extension, is unequivocal (see Figure 1.11). Another gridiron extension from the same period, but this time following an 1860s plan by Hobrecht for Berlin, introduced tightly knit rectangular tenement blocks. The density of accommodation, combined with inadequate ventilation or open space, provided ammunition for campaigners and modernisers who simultaneously equated both the medieval block and the 19th century European grid, and by extension the urban block, as a symptom of urban deprivation and misery.

Contrasting dramatically with Berlin's cramped apartment blocks, the city of Copenhagen responded to its housing shortage with far larger urban blocks, following a planned extension drawn up by its City Engineer, Charles Ambt, towards the end of the 19th century. These 'mega blocks' comprised a more or less continuous perimeter of apartments surrounding a generous shared open space.[18] Whereas the planned extensions to Berlin and Barcelona comprised smaller blocks that were then further subdivided into individual building plots, it is noteworthy that the entirety of the blocks are occupied by single buildings, rather than being subdivided into plots. Although this is not unusual in Copenhagen, it is rare in 19th century masterplanning. In some instances the austere 'street wall' (i.e. the outside face of the block) hides a courtyard with the proportions of a city park. Also contrasting with the traditional (outward-facing) perimeter block, the outer 'public' face is not distinguished here from the inner 'private' one, and the internal layout of apartments allows residents freedom of choice over whether to occupy the 'front' rooms as living spaces and the backs as bedrooms, or vice versa. Rather than adopting a rigorous gridiron plan, and following criticism that his initial plan was too boring, Ambt's masterplan is more wilfully shaped than a standard grid, with changes in the alignments of streets (see Figure 1.12). The result is more lozenge- or trapezoid-shaped blocks. Taking these characteristics together – the shared access to green space and the 'planned picturesque' – the Ambt plan can be read as combining elements of garden city thinking (in particular its association of green space with healthy living) with aspects of the traditional urban block (a perimeter of buildings surrounded by a connected network of streets).

As in Copenhagen, the Dutch city of Amsterdam also took a hands-on role in addressing its shortage of affordable housing at the turn of the 20th century. The government passed a housing act in 1901 that required municipalities to clear slums and to establish masterplanned extensions with the express purpose of providing affordable housing either directly or through housing associations.[19] Like Ambt's plan for Copenhagen, Berlage's more extensive masterplan for South Amsterdam (see Figure 1.12) echoes both Baroque principles on the one hand (an evident concern with axes, perspective and promenades), and the principles of the Garden City Movement taking root in the UK on the other (provision of public open spaces as well as private gardens and 'breathing space' for its inhabitants). The dwellings themselves, comprising stacked apartments, with the interior of the block given over to private gardens owned by the ground floor residents, were not innovative in a Dutch context, although the early modernist expression of the architecture (not designed by Berlage himself) speaks to an emerging tension between a modernist aesthetic and traditional approaches to masterplanning.

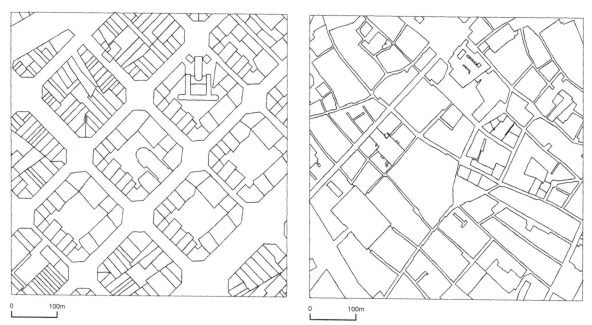

0   100m

1.11 (Left) Barcelona post-Cerdà. (Right) The medieval core, unaffected by Cerdà.

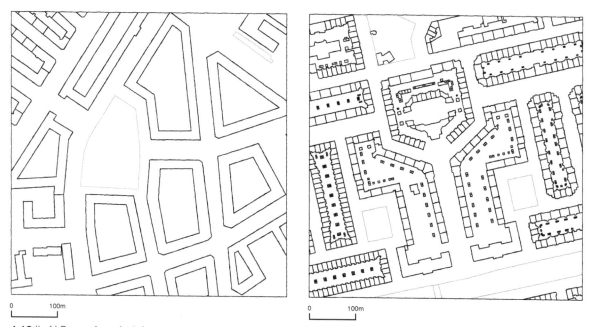

0   100m

1.12 (Left) Extract from Ambt's masterplan for Copenhagen. (Right) Extract from Berlage's masterplan for South Amsterdam.

THE BLOCK IN COLONIAL AFRICA AND ARABIA

Alongside physical factors, there are more nuanced, social, economic and cultural forces which shape the block, as seen in the contrast between urban block formation in Western culture and Muslim culture, and the impact of Western masterplanning ideas on that culture. This is most easily illustrated with reference to a traditional Arabic urban structure typified by the Medina, Marrakech, where narrow derbs give access to a limited number of courtyard houses (see Figure 1.13). These groupings are based on familial, tribal and ethnic divisions and predicated on the requirement in Islamic religious law to shield women from view. Here, the narrow, dead-end lanes serve to restrict through access and subtle changes in direction are combined with the walled enclosure of the courtyard dwellings that simultaneously provide shade from the sun and shield their inhabitants from unwanted intrusion.

The residential clusters themselves formed semi-autonomous social units – a kind of introverted superblock – each establishing and controlling their own local mosque, hamam, bakery and shared street fountains.

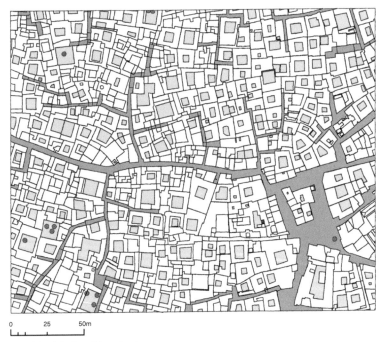

0   25   50m

1.13 The Medina, Marrakech.

The modern Arabic city is much harder to read. Yasser Elsheshtawy notes in 'Urban Dualities in the Arab World' that '...it is a setting where one can observe the tensions of modernity and tradition; religiosity and secularism; exhibitionism and veiling; in short a place of contradictions and paradoxes'.[20] Modern Arabic cities such as Doha and Dubai are a product of globalisation as much as anything else.

Reliant on a large immigrant labour force, segregation remains a feature, but this is manifested in less subtle ways: the native population occupying gated compounds and the remainder occupying shanty towns.

In another African city – Ouagadougou in Burkina Faso – French colonisers at the turn of the 20th century imposed a rational grid, but as shown in Figure 1.14, these were walled in and occupied by traditional round mud huts, highlighting the somewhat farcical imposition of one culture's agenda over another.

Following independence, the ruling government employed Dutch town planners led by Coen Beeker to replace informal settlements with a new masterplan that would regularise land holdings and provide sanitary drainage conditions. Figure 1.15 is redrawn from a survey by Beeker[21] and at first glance reads as an 'organic' settlement of irregular but connected blocks. As such it differs from the Medina (which is more impermeable) but on closer examination, the 'blocks' are composed of enclosed compounds containing small makeshift dwellings. The masterplanned grid, in contrast, reads as a wholly rational grid of blocks subdivided into equal plots (Figures 1.16 and 1.17). The intervention was politically successful but it is unclear whether it owed its success to the masterplan or the fact that the people were provided with sanitary drainage and a legitimate stake-holding in their plot. Suffice to say the masterplan creates outward-facing plots where previously there were inward-facing ones, taking no cues from its informal predecessor.

1.14 Aerial view of Ouagadougou taken by Walter Mittelholzer during the early 1930s.

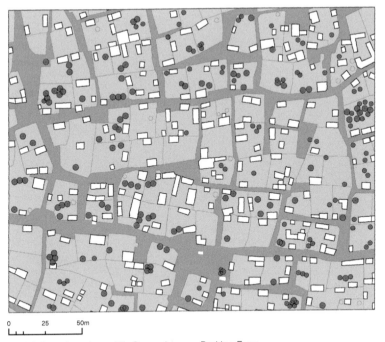

0 25 50m

1.15 Informal settlement in Ouagadougou, Burkina Faso.

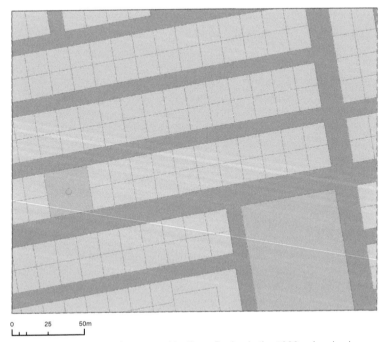

0 25 50m

1.16 The Dutch masterplan, created by Coen Beeker in the 1980s, showing how the informal settlement was re-planned..

1.17 The same area of Ouagadougou as viewed from above.

THE MODERN BLOCK

The 20th century witnessed a concerted move away from the traditional urban block in favour of new approaches to urban form: notably high-density freestanding point blocks and high-density slab blocks, alongside lower-density forms that separated car movement from pedestrians. Both approaches eroded the relationship of the block to the street associated with traditional urban blocks, and both ultimately failed. Towards the latter part of the century into the 21st century, as realisation dawned that the widespread social and environmental problems associated with many such developments were in large part attributable to the urban forms themselves, attention once again returned to the positive qualities of traditional urban forms – especially perimeter urban blocks – which began to be reasserted in urban design theory and practice. A more persistent trend – suburbanisation – also affected the fortunes of the block, with subtle yet longer-lasting and more widespread effects.

In the early part of the century the population of Britain's major cities and towns, especially London, continued to grow apace and their demand for housing was accommodated through the ongoing construction of speculatively built estates, very much in the mode of operation already established by the Georgian estate builders.

The resultant inner suburbs comprised monotonous blocks of row housing, however, attracting negative attention following World War II. Ironically, areas of by-law housing that survived both the war and later slum clearance proved their enduring appeal (once internal plumbing became available) by also surviving their intended replacement – the tower block – in many cases.

In contrast to the urban extensions masterplanned for Copenhagen and Amsterdam, the Garden City Movement in Britain favoured a more overtly 'suburban' model. Initiated in Britain by Ebenezer Howard at the turn of the 19th century and realised in the 20th century, the movement was an altruistic response to the conditions associated with overcrowding, fuelled by a vision to combine the benefits of town and country living and working together in the form of new self-contained satellite towns. Consisting essentially of a diagram, his ideas found expression in the creation of new towns and suburbs by architects Parker and Unwin at Letchworth, Welwyn and Hampstead, respectively, and consequently exerted a long-lasting influence on the design of new suburban blocks: based loosely on perimeter blocks but comprising low-density single-family dwellings with individual private gardens instead of apartment blocks.

Unwin's initial sketch masterplan for Hampstead sought to group as many houses as possible around a park, with views of Hampstead Heath. This was to be achieved using one of Parker and Unwin's core design ideas: the close. This innovation, the forerunner of the modern cul-de-sac, combined with a clear hierarchy of entrance, centre, axis, landmark and edge, provided a clear spatial organisation. Another 'innovation' of garden suburb 'block' design saw the introduction of shared allotment gardens in the interior of some of its blocks (see Figure 1.18). This recalls the structure of the medieval block, where market gardening was a necessity, and harks back to the rural ideal of the movement for self-sufficiency. With the added input of an extension of the original plan to the north-east by Edward Lutyens, a monumental square with radiating boulevards introduced a flavour of Baroque grandeur that overwhelms the planned picturesque of the original masterplan, and seems out of scale with its domestically scaled urban fabric.[22]

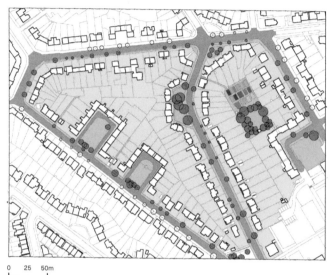

0   25   50m

1.18 Part of Hampstead Garden Suburb showing the loose perimeter block structure, folded to create closes and enclosing allotment gardens.

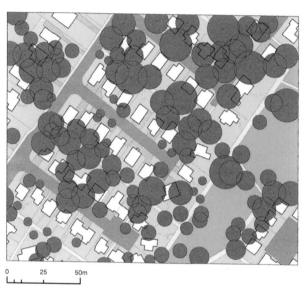

0   25   50m

1.19 Plan of a Radburn block, New Jersey showing segregation of car and pedestrian movement (note: houses shown indicatively).

The Garden City Movement manifested itself in other forms throughout Europe and North America. For example, the New York Regional Planning Association formulated a plan incorporating Clarence Perry's ideas for neighbourhood units centred on a primary school and community centre, serving a neighbourhood population of around 5000 people. The concept discouraged through traffic and its principles were taken a step further by Clarence Stein and Henry Wright's built proposals for a new suburb in Radburn, New Jersey (see Figure 1.19).[23]

Their 1928 plan for Radburn responded to rising levels of car traffic and the danger this posed to children. Writing in 1957, Stein suggested that the prevailing level of car traffic rendered the gridiron street pattern '...as obsolete as the fortified town wall'.[24] He observed that the roadbed was the children's main play space, and that the grid made all streets equally inviting to traffic, as well as subjecting pedestrians to 20 risky street crossings per mile.

The essence of the Radburn strategy was to impose a hierarchy of roads serving different categories of road users: service roads for direct access to house clusters (dead-end streets); secondary collector roads around the edges of the superblocks; through roads linking neighbourhoods; and highways for connection to the outside world. This involved separating pedestrian movement from car movement and turning the internal planning of houses around so that habitable rooms (living rooms and bedrooms) would face the pedestrian walkways while service rooms (kitchens, utility rooms, garages and bathrooms) would face the access roads. Each house cluster/cul-de-sac was separated by a pedestrian path linking the collector roads to a centralised linear park. The plan for Radburn was not fully implemented in New Jersey but enough of it was completed by 1930 for the rest of the world to take notice.

Interrupted by World War II and following the widespread destruction of many urban areas, new rationalist planning ideas based on the separation of four main functions – living, working, recreation and transport – were promulgated by the Athens Charter, which emerged from the Congrès Internationaux d'Architecture Moderne (CIAM) held in 1933 (published a decade later by Le Corbusier) and were widely adopted by planners and architects in their plans for reconstruction and rehousing worldwide.

Two parallel thought processes further affected block layouts: firstly, the segregation of pedestrians from cars; secondly, the creation of self-contained mid- or high-rise point blocks that would accommodate the masses served by 'streets in the air' (a term coined to describe deck-access housing). Thus, in post-war Britain new development tended to manifest itself in one of two ways: high-rise residential towers in urban areas, and low-rise estates following Radburn principles in suburban areas, including new towns such as Stevenage and Hemel Hempstead.

Le Corbusier's theoretical projects for freestanding towers and slabs such as his 'Plan Voisin' and 'Ville Radieuse' produced in the 1930s, and his built work such as the Unité d'Habitation in Marseille, which included an enclosed internal street on the 5th floor, inspired numerous like-minded schemes such as the Highpoint Towers built in 1933 (designed by the Tecton Group) and the meandering Park Hill development in Sheffield (designed by Jack Lynn and Ivor Smith). But applied to damper climates, with poor connections and occupied by disadvantaged communities, they created the perfect conditions for communities to fester and ultimately disintegrate, creating a new kind of slum scenario with residents dislocated from the city and deprived of any of the benefits of city life.

Whereas Le Corbusier's Unité block attempted to internalise the street, British versions tended to move the access ways back to the outside of the building. Both versions elevated themselves from the ground plane and thereby negated the traditional relationship of dwelling to street found in traditional row blocks or perimeter blocks. Although the back-to-back slum dwellings replaced by Park Hill were notoriously squalid and crime-ridden, Park Hill also declined, and lay vacant and vandalised for many years before being taken on as a presently ongoing regeneration project by Urban Splash (Figures 1.20 and 1.21).

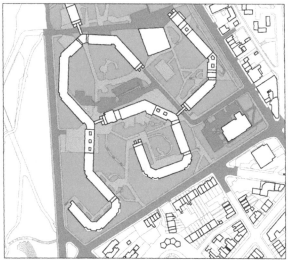

0   25   50m

1.20 Partial plan of the Park Hill block, Sheffield, showing the loose enclosure of shared spaces.

1.21 Aerial view of the Park Hill blocks.

The publication of the influential Traffic in Towns report in the UK by Colin Buchanan in 1963 set the scene for a new response to the growing problem of traffic congestion along similar lines as the Radburn estate more than 30 years earlier. The Buchanan Report posited that traffic is generated by occupation of buildings, yet historic towns are not able to accommodate either traffic that has business in the town, or traffic that is attempting to pass through it. Buchanan recognised that accessibility alone wasn't the problem. Cars also generated noise, fumes, 'intimidation' and visual intrusion and he pointed out that the ability to walk around the town unfettered by these intrusions amounted to '...a useful guide to the civilised quality of an urban area.'[25] Following this line of reasoning the report proposed the concept of 'environmental areas' comprising discrete cells that would be protected from through traffic by imposing a hierarchical network of primary, district and local distributor roads. Buchanan described this arrangement, saying: 'The system may be likened to the trunk, limbs, branches, and finally the twigs (corresponding to the access roads) of a tree.'[26]

Buchanan realised that such a system required 'comprehensive' intervention over a wide area and already sensed that the opportunity to impose such solutions on existing town centres would be hampered by their ongoing development. The idea gained a great deal of traction in the planning of new towns and new suburbs, and had significant implications for block-based planning.

One such example, New Ash Green in Kent, designed by the architect Eric Lyons and built in the late 1960s, illustrates the idea manifested in a more subtle way than Radburn, but with similar implications to the housing accessed by cul-de-sacs leading to garages and parking courts served by a distributor road (see Figure 1.22). The backs of the houses are oriented to the parking areas and the fronts face towards linear green spaces, linked by pedestrian-only pathways. Here, the landscape is given primary importance, and wraps the block as well as insinuating itself through them. What is singularly different from the Radburn layout (and evident in numerous other 'Radburn-type' layouts around the UK and elsewhere) is that the individual house plots do not directly line the access road. This fundamental difference in form is reinforced by the fact that whereas the house plots lining the Radburn cul-de-sacs are clearly visible across their low-fenced property boundaries, the ones at New Ash Green and most similar developments are enclosed by high and impermeable fences. These two factors together effectively isolate the access roads from direct lines of sight and are criticised as an inherent problem with the urban form, because the parking areas and segregated pathways are vulnerable to antisocial behaviours.

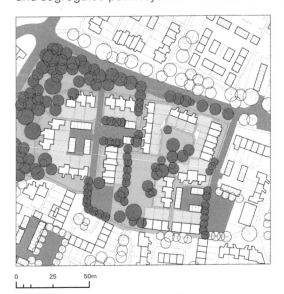

0   25   50m

1.22 Partial plan of New Ash Green, Kent.

THE POST-MODERN BLOCK

These different examples of urban form demonstrate some of the thinking that influenced a concerted shift away from the idea of the traditional urban or perimeter block as an urban form to be followed, much less celebrated. But a pushback did occur, and one that – directly or indirectly – did lead to a 'root and branch' reappraisal of those urban structures that emerged from the Athens Charter, which segregated land-use zoning and trends in both suburban and urban development, and favoured the cul-de-sac, courtyard block and the point block over its perimeter block forebears.

Jane Jacobs railed at the ongoing attempts by North American planners to 'improve' the urban environment along the lines advocated by CIAM in her famous book of 1961 *The Death and Life of Great American Cities*. Jacobs was primarily interested in street life, rather than the block, but realised that the size and shape of blocks in her native New York were critical factors in generating or stifling the potential for street life to occur, stating: 'Long blocks, in their nature, thwart the potential advantages that cities offer to incubation, experimentation, and many small or special enterprises, insofar as these depend on drawing their customers or clients from among much larger cross-sections of passing public.'[27]

The British-American architect and design theorist Christopher Alexander issued another broadside in 1972, deconstructing Buchanan's idea that designing urban areas in the model of a tree, with different levels of hierarchy and segregation of uses and modes of transport, is a 'good idea'. Alexander argued that the 'natural city' is not a tree, but a semi-lattice, comprising overlaps of numerous different phenomena that cumulatively add up to more than the sum of their parts. Alexander decries the 'tree-like' features of several city plans and suburbs, including criticism of the idea of the neighbourhood as a self-contained unit, the superblock, separation of functions, segregation of play into enclosures and the segregation of cars from pedestrians.

Further attacks on the functionalist orthodoxy of urban thinking followed soon after. The civil rights movement in the USA challenged racist agendas behind certain programmes of urban renewal and highways construction. Feminists began to critique the sexist assumptions underlying the creation of urban (and suburban) and domestic space. Meanwhile environmentalists were increasingly challenging the polluting and alienating effects of car traffic.[28] Oscar Newman's concept of 'defensible space' (published in 1973) lent statistical evidence to the issues that Jacobs might have felt intuitively: crime was more likely to occur in the spaces between buildings for which no one felt responsible, compared to the public streets that bordered them.[29] His treatise recommended that the distinction between public and private spaces should be unambiguous and, in so doing, served to undermine planners' confidence in the point block as a housing model. Alice Coleman's 'Utopia on Trial' was published in 1985 and mapped the occurrence of antisocial behaviour across 4099 blocks of flats and 4172 individual houses. Importantly, she stressed that the higher incidence of crime associated with high-rise flats was not correlated with indices of deprivation or unemployment.[30] This statistical study confirmed the previously held conjecture that the ambiguous urban spaces surrounding point block configurations were socially problematic by design.

Writing at the same time, in 1973, Nicholas Taylor did for the inner London suburb what Jacobs did for Greenwich Village and Manhattan. His book *The Village in the City* extolled the virtues of the terraced house: its mediation of public and private space, together with '...the effortless ability of the traditional back yard to absorb on equal terms the baby's pram, the toddler's toys, the housewife's washing lines and the dog's kennel, every one of them closely overlooked from the kitchen'.[31]

Typifying the West's disenchantment with the kind of wholesale regeneration characteristic of many post-war projects, Berlin's International Building Exhibition (IBA) in 1984–1987 advocated a departure from modernist towers and slabs, and a return to a more sensitive and contextual approach based on the perimeter block and referencing the city's pre-existing urban morphology. Formally, its objective was to reinstate the function of the block as the 'anonymous' urban fabric of the city punctuated by individual civic buildings, which gain symbolic importance by contrast to this anonymity, while reinstating the role of the street as the 'theatre' of public life. Rob Krier's plan for Ritterstrasse (see Figure 1.23) followed the building line and height of the adjacent 19th century blocks but was further subdivided with internal courtyards and crossed by pedestrian streets.[32] The resulting block form, which is made up of 35 individual buildings by six different architectural practices, clearly articulates a hierarchy of space from the public life of the street grid, semi-public internal streets and private courtyards.

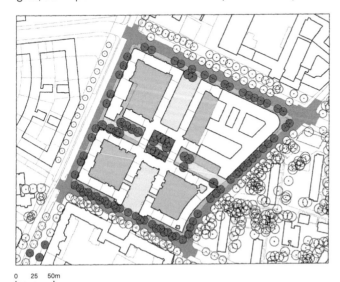

0   25   50m

1.23 Block at Ritterstrasse, Berlin.

In the USA, the New Urbanism movement also looked to the past to recreate a sense of neighbourhood and community it felt was destroyed by post-war suburbanisation. While the built projects espousing the tenets of New Urbanism have been criticised for their nostalgia (and being aimed at the affluent), they were nonetheless radical for seeking to create 'walkable' and accessible neighbourhoods formed of small blocks in place of disconnected cul-de-sacs, and in this way at least tried to create the preconditions for communities to form by themselves.

While their projects have also been criticised for lacking 'urbanity', projects such as Battery Park in New York did in fact facilitate buildings by different architects and developers (provided they followed prescribed guidelines in the form of a design code). Allowing for this precondition to urbanity to be 'built in' to the masterplan, albeit in a watered-down format, should not be downplayed.

The New Urbanists consolidated their principles in the Charter of the New Urbanism published in 1999. The principles are articulated across three scales: the city/town; neighbourhood/district/corridor (used to describe connectors of neighbourhoods or districts, e.g. avenues); and block/street/building. In this last category the principles advocate the physical definition of streets that are safe, pedestrian-friendly and accessible.[33] In doing so, they avoid referring to specific block types, but the avoidance of cul-de-sac forms or gated developments is implicit.

Failing urban centres combined with sprawling commuter belts in Britain prompted the then Labour government to commission an 'Urban Task Force' led by Richard Rogers. Its 1999 report[34] was primarily aimed at regenerating urban areas but advocated urban design principles informed by traditional cities and suburbs. A recurring theme of the report is the importance of permeability and accessibility to place-making, referencing the New Urbanists' critique of cul-de-sac suburban forms, and the failure of modernist slab and point blocks to create attractive or safe streets. The report influenced design policy in many areas including the subsequent publication of *Planning Policy Guidance Note 3: Housing (PPG3)*, promoting higher density housing, *By Design: Urban Design in the Planning System*, and *The Urban Design Compendium*, promoting 'best practice' in urban design, all published in 2000. *The Urban Design Compendium* is notable in this regard because it widened the discussion from general urban design principles to include specific guidance promoting perimeter block types.[35]

Separately, these various projects, movements and manifestos project a somewhat bewildering array of ideas and agendas. Taken together, they demonstrate an emerging consensus that low-density suburbs based on cul-de-sacs, alongside high-density urban development based on slab and point blocks, needed to be rethought, and that the solution lies in traditional urban forms. It highlights the continued relevance of the urban block and the street, and the importance of bringing the perimeter block back to the forefront of urban design thinking. The continued relevance of the plot to the block and street remains somewhat overlooked, however, leading us to assert that the (traditional) urban block is dead, long live the block!

DEFINING THE BLOCK

Having outlined a brief history of the block and some of the theories underpinning different approaches to designing blocks, it's important to understand how this relates to contemporary urban design and ways it might be applied to how we design now, which requires a more forensic dissection of block types.

This chapter sets out a 'taxonomy' of urban forms – block types – describing various options for any given parcel of land, of which the 'perimeter block' is just one configuration. The relationship of different block types to their surrounding street network is touched upon for each example. It also refers to urban forms that are not 'blocks' in the strict sense of the word, but are central to our understanding of the block, or are found in hybridised forms of blocks.

TERMINOLOGY

The block is described by the *Urban Design Compendium* as the land area defined by the grid of streets: 'It can vary considerably in shape and size according to the configuration of streets, preferred orientation and topography, for instance, as well as the nature of plot subdivisions and building types that are to be accommodated.'[1]

The development of the land enclosed within the block boundary can then be interpreted in a variety of ways. The list of potential physical configurations below sets out a taxonomy of basic forms that an urban block layout might take on. These have been organised into five different block types, and a further section on related urban forms, which includes three significant variants of block design that form the basis of some hybrid block types. Each of the block types (or other urban forms) has both an exterior face – usually to the public street, but sometimes to a private street or yard – and a semi-public/private interior within the block itself:

     A – The perimeter block
     B – The row block
     C – The point block
     D – The ribbon block
     E – The courtyard block
     F – Other variants of urban form
        Court
        Close
        Cul-de-sac

The list of types has been arranged on the basis of a rough spectrum, extending from public-facing through to private-facing.

The 'street' is the space that is made manifest by the thresholds between public and private space, and its success as a place in its own right (as opposed to its functionality as a conduit for movement) depends to a very large extent on the design of the blocks themselves: the way the blocks are arranged in relation to their neighbours, and the control of their edge conditions. This is true for all listed block types and urban forms however, it is precisely the degree to which any given configuration engages with the public realm in general, and the street in particular, that is key.

The merits and compromises involved in designing each of these block types or forms will be considered here, as well as ways that they might merge and hybridise. As with any taxonomy, the definition of types is useful only in so far as it imposes order across a range of forms that can in some way be identified as being different from one another. In reality, it is rare to find two blocks that are exactly the same, and the intention is to aid understanding rather than to compartmentalise design thinking. As such, some existing blocks are 'pure' versions of the types listed, while others are more difficult to categorise. These function as hybrids, sharing characteristics between one or more types. It is the complexity of the consequent relationships these oscillations of form set up in the social realm that makes the study of urban form so fascinating.

The discussions that follow revolve around a series of simplified diagrams, and corresponding photo examples, each illustrating the main features of the type (or sub-type). For simplicity's sake, the diagrams adopt orthogonal shapes. This should not be taken to infer that the discussion only relates to orthogonal types. Blocks can (and often do) take on warped or distorted shapes to respond to the lie of the land, pre-existing forms, natural constraints or the whim of the designer.

2.1 Contemporary perimeter block, Den Haag, the Netherlands.

BLOCK TYPES

A – THE PERIMETER BLOCK

The term 'perimeter block' is thought to have originated with Bentley et al.'s influential manual for designers, *Responsive Environments: A Manual for Designers*, first published in 1985.[2] Based on the premise that 'all buildings need two faces: a *front* onto public space, for entrances and most public activities, and a *back* where the most private activities can go', they pointed out that, applied consistently, the front/back distinction leads to a type of layout that they called 'perimeter block development'.

The defining characteristic of the perimeter block identified by the *Urban Design Compendium* is that the edges of the block are lined with buildings. According to the *Compendium*, this is the best way to accommodate a diversity of building types and uses at medium to high densities, while ensuring that building frontages relate positively to the public realm.[3] The 'pure' perimeter block, with an unbroken or continuous lining, is relatively rare; it is unusual to find an urban block with no breaks or gaps and a consistently outward-facing set of façades. The idiosyncrasies of the perimeter block and its departures from a 'pure form' are interesting to ponder as these will have been determined by a broad range of social, practical and economic demands, and will concurrently influence these demands.

The accessible relationship of the perimeter block to its urban context is probably its most important feature from an urban designer's point of view. Strategically placing primary entrances on the street façade animates the street with the comings and goings of inhabitants, while locating living/working spaces increases the visibility of daily activity within the block and reinforces the sense of surveillance that overlooking of the street creates. The street benefits greatly from these features, although achieving a good design for the rear or inner core is more complex.

The tussle between the outer and inner domains of the block is set up inadvertently by its form, but quickly becomes the primary consideration for the designer who needs to negotiate an appropriate line between the push and pull factors of achieving an active street or an active inner court. This negotiation, and the impetus on the designer to resolve fronts and backs, fuels an almost exponential cascade of alternative configurations in the ongoing attempt to achieve that ideal harmonious balance between the humming and dynamic street and the encouragement of the cosy community within the block.

Much of this negotiation hinges on decision-making regarding the location of entrances, and the placement of occupied live/work spaces that will overlook the exterior or interior terrain. If all the entrances and living spaces are placed on the outer perimeter, then the street will be active and overlooked while the inner court will become a back-of-house zone that feels neglected. If all the entrances are on the inside of the block, it ceases to be defined as a perimeter block and is operating as a courtyard block instead. Achieving a happy balance of outer and inner activity, with a focus on a more publicly oriented outer edge, is a significant design challenge.

There is a general consensus that the outward-facing configuration of perimeter blocks has significant social benefits for the life of the street. It does, however, generate some important design implications, especially for the identity of the block itself. The primacy given to the streetscape means that the inhabitant's experience of entering their 'dwelling' is through their own side of the block, and from the space of the street itself, which is defined by their façade of the block and the façade of the block opposite: they are therefore less cognizant of the sides of the block they do not frequent, and more aware of the character/identity of the street that they enter their dwelling from. The homogeneity of the block itself as an entity with its own identity is therefore conditional in the perimeter block configuration (as opposed to, say, the courtyard or square), because its edges/sides (usually three or four) are never perceived at the same time.

Promotion of the street as the main urban 'living space' has a long and relatively successful history. Where cities have grown incrementally on the basis of small plots of land, the approach of designing from the streetscape back is systematically viable, but it can be much more challenging in the contemporary context.

The ownership of parcels of land is usually organised by block, meaning that the blocks themselves are often designed/commissioned/built independently of one another, while the space between them (the street) is not subjected to the same design scrutiny, the upshot being that the designer or designers of the block are ultimately only considering the design of one-half of the streetscape edges, while it is the interaction of these opposing edges that will ultimately determine the success of the street as a whole. The designer(s) of the block may not particularly value their role as an urban intermediary, and they may not be aware of – or responsive to – the fact that they are designing four (–/+) different perimeters that are fronting onto four potentially very different streets. This aspect of perimeter block design is, however, important for the designer to take on board, especially in terms of the alternative psychological 'territories' that outward-facing blocks engender and, crucially, their diminished control in defining these.

There are, however, often ways of ameliorating this situation. On larger developments of multiple blocks, for instance, the overall masterplan may include a design code and/or a public realm design that serves to coordinate design across the ownership divide. Splitting the ownership or development parcels of the whole block into smaller plots of individual or grouped/phased developments can also more effectively emulate the way streetscapes emerged historically. Plot-based approaches to development have gained popularity in Germany (e.g. Tubingen, Vauban and Rieselfeld near Freiburg) and the Netherlands (Ijburg in Amsterdam, Homerusquartier, Almere), particularly where land is publicly owned. Although this was once the default setting for traditional urban planning, plot-based development in a contemporary setting usually involves a far greater amount of coordination than orthodox approaches to property development are prepared to facilitate, and relies on an acceptance that the development will not be 'finished' all at once. This is at once its strength and its potential weakness.

A1 – PERIMETER BLOCK WITH BACK-TO-BACK PLOTS

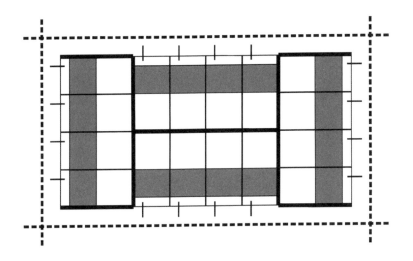

2.2 Perimeter block with back-to-back plots (diagram).

One of the simplest forms of perimeter block is that of four rows that are placed back to back. By 'turning' the plots to address each edge of the block, there are no entirely blank gabled edges, although consideration given to side entrances or fenestration on houses that turn corners can greatly improve the urban offer. This type has no shared 'inner core', so the primacy of the relationship of the accommodation to the street is a given, and there is little sense of its own identity. Rather identity is generated by enclosure of the street between facing blocks.

Potential for mixed use is constrained due to the lack of rear access and narrow street frontage. In traditional Victorian neighbourhoods, it is commonplace to find corner shops that have been converted from single-family dwellings, allowing the proprietor to live over the shop. Figure 2.2 implies a perimeter block composed of individual house plots, each with a front and rear garden. This arrangement is common, but the same principles apply to plots comprising, for example, individual apartment buildings or office buildings, with or without gardens to the front and/or back.

Moving up in scale, the relationship between the outer edge of the perimeter block and the space defined within it alters somewhat. To achieve higher densities and mixed uses, housing may take the form of apartments and/or shops, offices or live/work units. The ground floor apartments may have rear gardens or the interior of the block may be taken up entirely by communal space – open space, car parking or both. Increasing the dimensions of the block also increases the usable size of the inner space it encloses, thereby gaining an accessible interior domain with a new secondary 'frontage' overlooking it with consequent budgetary implications.

The configurations of larger-scale versions of the perimeter block are probably endless, but the main types are identified in the following subsections.

2.3 Suburban perimeter block with back-to-back plots.

2.4 Urban perimeter block with back-to-back plots.

A2 – PERIMETER BLOCK WITH UNINHABITED COURTYARD

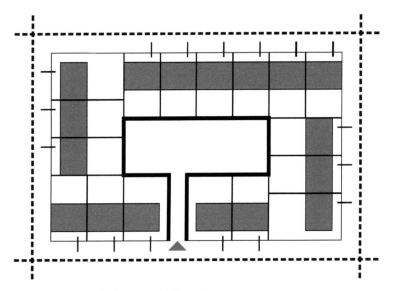

2.5 Perimeter block with uninhabited courtyard (diagram).

Key Features

- Clear definition of the street
- Dilutes activation of the street as car users tend to rely on access from rear courtyard
- Provides for allocated parking within rear court, without reliance on on-street parking
- Rear courts are often poorly overlooked with ambiguous responsibility for maintenance resulting in spaces that are neglected and/or prone to misuse

Design Challenges

- Imbuing the rear court area with a sense of place and sense of shared ownership
- Managing security and refuse storage/collection
- Addressing the street corners

The perimeter block with uninhabited rear courtyard is relatively common (see Figure 2.5). In relation to the English Garden Suburbs of the early 20th century, some blocks were provided with allotment gardens. In more recent times, with the growth in car ownership, the type mutated to accommodate car parking within the courtyard. Due to its vulnerability to misuse, this rear domain is often gated for use as a controlled parking court for inhabitants of the block. On a positive note, the type removes the need to provide parking on the street or on-plot parking accessed from the street. This is useful if there are reasons why it is expedient to limit multiple driveways from the street, but the street nevertheless suffers if the car users then opt to enter their properties via the back gate, in which case the usage and status of the front door is undermined, and the street is deprived of activity. The quality of this rear domain is often low, given its use as a car park, bin storage, secondary façades – or even blank fencing – facing onto it, and the prohibitive cost of providing good lighting or CCTV.

A3 – PERIMETER BLOCK WITH INHABITED COURTYARD

Key Features

- Less clear definition of street structure; semi-public through routes may be introduced
- Direct overlooking of the semi-public realm within the block is achieved through locating some units within the rear courts
- Allows for allocated parking within rear court areas, whilst avoiding the pitfalls associated with the uninhabited courtyard solution
- Less space-efficient due to the complexity of achieving such configurations

Design Challenges

- Achieving a balance of front of block vs back of block that affords units within rear courts an attractive/ marketable setting
- Retaining an active street front

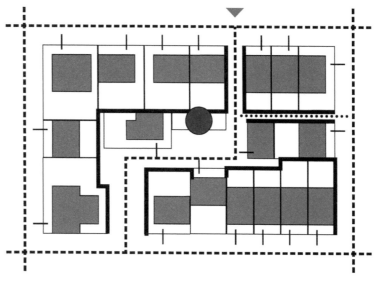

2.6 Perimeter block with inhabited courtyard (diagram).

The perimeter block with an inhabited courtyard is an interesting variant of this type (see Figure 2.6). Here, some accommodation is included within the rear court itself, which presents the advantages of higher-quality primary façades fronting onto the space and the passive surveillance entailed, while also offering a sense of alternative character and identity to this quieter off-street domain. The rear courtyard basically becomes an extension of a hierarchical street network, which allows the management and maintenance to be centralised, giving flexibility in the ownership model for the development. Poundbury in Dorset has successfully instituted inhabited rear courts incorporating pedestrian 'lanes', as discussed in more detail later on.

2.7 Inhabited courtyard at Poundbury, Dorset.

A4 – PERIMETER BLOCK WITH COMMUNAL COURTYARD

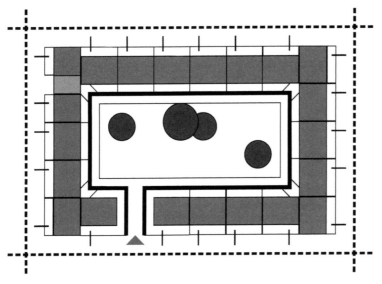

2.8 Closed perimeter block with communal courtyard (diagram).

Key Features

- Clear orientation of public fronts to street with private/semi-private backs oriented towards communal space within the block interior
- Opening a publicly accessible route through the block increases permeability, though at the expense of perceived security and collective ownership
- Quality of communal space is often compromised by parking requirements, either surface or undercroft

Design Challenges

- Striking a balance between communal vs private gardens and the interface between them is a key design challenge for this variant

The perimeter block that encloses a communal amenity area or garden is popular. This is often used by blocks containing apartments and/or mixed-use accommodation, where residents benefit from a shared garden space, akin to that of a courtyard block. The rear accommodation benefits from views over greenery. The model can also be achieved by mixing single houses with private rear gardens along some or all of its edges.

The courtyard/garden itself might either be 'closed' (see Figure 2.8) or 'open', allowing for a pedestrian route through it (see Figure 2.9). If many of these open block types are located adjacent to one another, it can contribute to a separate network of pedestrian routes, which can be pleasant for achieving shortcuts and avoiding vehicular traffic, but draws people away from the main street network, to its detriment.

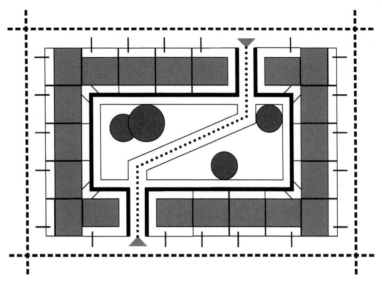

2.9 Open perimeter block with communal courtyard (diagram).

Funding the maintenance of this communal shared space requires careful consideration and usually needs to be centralised, which can restrict ownership options to some form of leasehold with associated maintenance charges. Encouraging a high usage of this space can be challenging due to its relative inaccessibility from dwellings. Direct rear access points should be included in order for the gardens to be well utilised, yet if these fall into general usage as main entrances, the street suffers from a reduction in activity.

The higher density of living associated with this type means that larger numbers of cars need to be accommodated. Where density is sufficiently high, the cost of providing car parking under the block can usually be justified. In out-of-town locations, however, it is more usual to find that the value/cost equation results in surface car parks within the block interior, at the expense of providing communal open space.

2.10 Example of a closed perimeter block with communal courtyard in Copenhagen, Denmark.

2.11 Aerial view of an open perimeter block with communal courtyard in Helsinki, Finland.

A5 – NESTED PERIMETER BLOCK

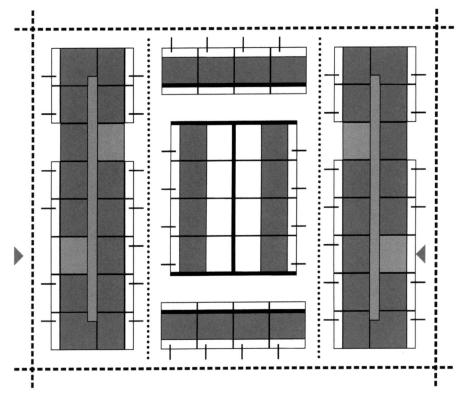

Key Features

- A block within a block, blurring the public/private movement hierarchy

- This type of configuration provides for intensification/ densification of use (potentially mixed use), although typically at the expense of open space

Design Challenges

- Resolving any privacy issues between backs and fronts of units, due to reduced separation distances involved in this configuration

2.12 'Nested' perimeter block (diagram).

Shifting away from the pure-form perimeter block towards more hybrid options may also offer some solutions. The 'nested' perimeter block (see Figure 2.12) is essentially a block within a block, with a densely occupied inner court. The diagram immediately suggests a number of advantages, offering a more nuanced and less polarised relationship between inner and outer, vehicular routes and pedestrian ways. This configuration is suggestive of row housing, although more permeable, and similar to the traditional row house with mews, although less obviously socially hierarchical. The varied accommodation lends itself to a diverse mix of uses and types of dwelling, while all the external habitable areas are overlooked and defensible to some extent. Outdoor amenity space is limited but could be expanded upon in alternative versions. Here, the benefits that more complex forms of hybrid configurations may offer in the creation of successful dwelling and working places become apparent.

2.13 Aerial view of a simple nested perimeter block in Stockholm, Sweden.

B – THE ROW BLOCK

Rows are one of the simplest ways of developing/configuring a block. The block form itself is not really 'designed' but emerges from the pragmatic, and economically expedient, placement of two rows of houses or buildings with front entrances and rear gardens, back to back. The buildings may be terraced, semi-detached or even detached, although in order to function as a 'block', the planning would be dense enough that the front façades would be visible and generally in alignment. The row block is well established, and although it has a mainly linear aspect and its purest version produces a rather rigid form, it is nevertheless important given its relative longevity and popularity with occupants and house-builders alike. Other more complex block types within the taxonomy are also likely to use 'rows' as a component of their set of parts.

The row's simplicity lies in the economies of scale of duplicating the same form along a single direction. However, this characteristic is also the reason for one of its main detractions, which lies in its relative inability to turn corners effectively, often leaving blank gables to the short edges of the block, and the consequent reduction in street quality that this engenders. The street network is active and overlooked by the fronts of dwellings or businesses in one direction, but can be austere and vulnerable to graffiti on the other. Given the linearity of the row, it also tends to march on indefinitely, especially where tight economics come into play. This encourages elongated block forms that can effectively become a barrier to permeability, or at the least define a directionality to the network that may or may not be appropriate.

This type has a wide range of applications and can also accommodate mixed uses through the tried and tested 'living over the shop' model, although this does alter marketability by omitting the direct relationship between the living accommodation and the rear garden. In the standard model, each building often ends up with two entrances (one residential and the other commercial), which has a positive impact on the interface with the street, given the amount of activity this generates along its primary edges.

Row housing as a type generally offers no (or little) shared public amenity space within the block form. This has the advantage that the public/private ownership boundaries are easy to surmise and navigate, whilst the requirement for the complication of an overarching management or ownership structure is avoided. The individual plots defined by each house and its garden can therefore easily be sold into private ownership, without any additional annual management fees charged to the freehold. This model therefore suits the home-owning aspirations of the British populace well – as well as its predilection for privacy.

In older neighbourhoods the traditional form of row housing relegates car parking to the street. Where parking is effectively in the public domain, it is therefore unallocated to any household, meaning that parking is available (or not) on a first-come, first-served basis. This arrangement works well in older suburban areas where there is no alternative available. However, in newer developments there is added value associated with an allocated car parking space. Further, the complexities of legally conveying a car parking space that is dislocated from the homeowner's plot induces pressure to provide for parking either on-plot to the front of houses (where they are terraced) or in between, meaning that the houses become separated, and consequently of lower density.

In past times, lower traffic volumes allowed the street to function as shared space, and 'doorstep play' for children. The volume of traffic experienced nowadays, however, tends to make the street unsafe as a communal space. Because this is not compensated for by an alternative shared space, it reduces the potential for those informal liaisons that help to establish a sense of local community.

B1 – THE ROW BLOCK WITH BACK-TO-BACK PLOTS

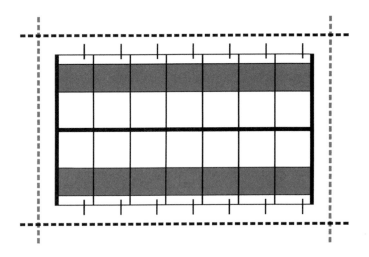

2.14 Row block with back-to-back plots diagram (diagram).

Row blocks are a simplified form of block where development is oriented to two sides of the block (usually the 'long' sides) but not the cross-streets (see Figure 2.14). It is therefore similar in type to the perimeter block with back-to-back plots, but only relates directly to the street along one axis. As such it is not a perimeter block in the strict sense, although it is commonly found in gridded masterplans.

The simplicity and efficiency of the row block has made it a popular choice for high-volume housing developments, but the relative limitations of its block formation for place-making should not be ignored. The type gives precedence to elongation along one axis (through adding additional units) over the other (through extending the length of gardens). This formation thus exposes undesirable short ends of a block along one axis, where blank gable ends and fences traditionally occur, compounded by over-extended monotonous terraces of units along the other axis. There are also practical issues with this tight-knit configuration, such as accessibility to rear gardens from the street, which must be either through the unit itself, or through a designated side passage (which may be shared between pairs of units, and/or built over at upper floor levels where retaining continuity of the terrace is required).

Some historic examples take the expediency of the row block to its ultimate conclusion, placing houses back-to-back without either an intervening open space for yards/gardens or a lane. This variation of the type has been rightly discredited for creating slum conditions and is rarely considered an option in contemporary urban planning practice. Instead, variations of this block with broken frontage (e.g. semi-detached housing) have tended to be favoured in

2.15 Aerial view showing a variety of row blocks, UK.

contemporary practice because they facilitate access to the side or rear more easily than row housing, but they are less space-efficient, producing less sustainable densities.

B2 – DUAL-ASPECT ROW WITH SERVICE LANE

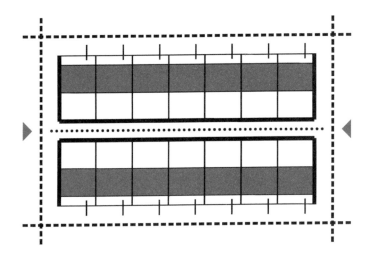

2.16 Dual-aspect row with service lane (diagram).

Key Features

- Efficient and economic form of block that lends itself to repetitive unit types and orthogonal forms
- Tends to push parking towards the street
- Lends itself to being elongated along one axis
- All units have ease of access to rear

Design Challenges

- Addressing the short side of the block (gable ends) and its relationship to the street network
- Avoiding monotony at the wider scale of the urban realm
- Ensuring the service lane is designed to be safe, secure and well maintained

From a practical point of view, the lack of rear access available in the traditional row block model is inconvenient for storage of bicycles and equipment, and if any works need doing to the rear of the houses or their gardens. Also, with no accessible 'back-of-house' area, household waste needs to be collected from the front of the dwellings, meaning that the streetscape is routinely occupied by refuse bins awaiting collection. For these reasons, a variant of the type evolved, incorporating a rear service lane (see Figure 2.16). The dual-aspect row type also adapts better to mixed use, by allowing service access and a back-of-house area for businesses at the rear.

Although it serves a useful purpose, the service lane is just that, and there is a tendency for them to be poorly maintained and often to attract antisocial behaviours. The lack of natural surveillance can also make them an attractive route for would-be burglars to gain access or escape undetected.

2.17 Aerial view of dual-aspect row block housing with service lane

B3 – THE MEWS BLOCK

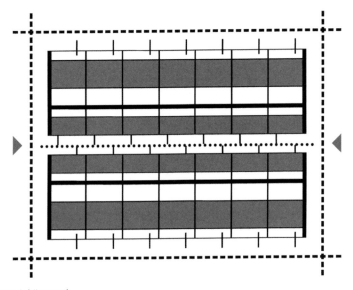

2.18 Mews block (diagram).

Key Features

- Entrances to units on the rear access lane in this variant legitimise public use of the mews, thus affording clear articulation of public and private realms
- Mews configuration introduces a hierarchy of movement but also potentially of land uses and unit size
- Allows for increased/filtered permeability

Design Challenges

- Addressing the street corners of the block and the entrance way(s) into the mews
- Where the street-facing units and mews-facing units occupy separate plots, facilitating access to the intervening open spaces

Whilst the row block is a versatile and efficient form of block design, its simplicity is self-limiting. To create the kind of active street network that urban designers and planners are striving for – one that is at once efficient, facilitates a range of land uses or different house types and sizes and is convivial along its edges – the row block needs to be more sophisticated. An interesting variant of the row block that achieves these aims, and with a long historical pedigree, is the mews block. Here, the rear access lane is itself fronted with a subsidiary set of buildings, traditionally occupying the rear of the same plot as the main street (see Figure 2.18). The mews lane usually runs right across the block, as shown in the diagram, but examples that are closed at one end also occur. The rear accommodation in a mews is different from the close in that it is an access way rather than an open space. It differs from the court in that the mews block is designed as a self-contained entity, where the front and rear buildings on a given plot have a direct and considered relationship both to one another (even if these have been divided later on), and to the street or mews respectively. In contrast, the court emerges historically from a more ad hoc process of subdividing an existing plot and infilling it with smaller buildings (usually small dwellings).

In its original form the mews offered a convenient way to serve a large family dwelling at the front. The development of the 'great estates' of London, Dublin and Edinburgh during the Georgian era made this form of block commonplace. The mews building was often referred to as a 'coach house', with living accommodation above for the driver or other domestic servants. With the growth of the middle classes and concurrent decline in the suitability of the house as a single-family dwelling, the type proved itself extremely adaptable to change. In higher-value areas, such as Belgravia in London, the main house lent itself to conversion to flats or offices (or in some cases continued occupation as a single-family dwelling), while the smaller mews building lent itself to single occupancy or live/work uses.

Meanwhile, in lower-value areas, such as the Gardiner Estate in north Dublin, the main houses frequently became slum dwellings and the mews buildings were occupied by low-grade commercial activities such as car repair workshops and their like. A contemporary renaissance of this type of mixed use can be seen in mews that are converted into live/work units.

2.19 Street view of a contemporary mews lane, Accordia, Cambridge, UK.

2.20 Street view of mews lane with former coach houses converted to residential use, London, UK.

C – THE POINT BLOCK

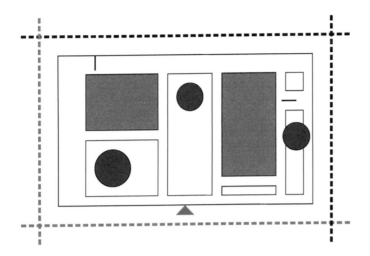

2.21 Point block (diagram).

The term point block needs unpacking, because it refers simultaneously to the form of the building (i.e. a building type) and a relationship to the area of land defined by streets on which it sits (our working definition of the block). Put together, the point block is generally understood to imply a freestanding building (or buildings) that occupies part of its own block, without enclosing the street in the way a traditional urban block does (see Figure 2.21). In some contexts, the term 'pavilion' or 'solitaire' is also used to identify this type. In traditional towns and cities, the type is usually reserved for civic buildings in prominent positions, such as churches or courts, and is thus distinguished from the general urban fabric. However, the modern movement in architecture also adopted the type – taking the form of residential towers or slabs – but isolating them from the surrounding fabric rather than integrating them.

The dilemma raised by pavilion and point blocks is that they generally have just one 'front'. The implication is that the relationship of the 'back' or 'sides' of the block to the public realm is less clear, and they cannot enclose streets in the same way as perimeter blocks or row blocks.

The relationship of the edges of the block to the street network is therefore of critical importance when it comes to assessing the merits of this type. A solitaire or pavilion block whose physical presence helps to define the edges of the street, either directly edging the street or with a narrow 'privacy' strip around it, can have a positive effect on the street network, especially if it has multiple entrances. Many civic and community buildings take the form of the pavilion or solitaire, so they are an important and timeless urban (and suburban) feature of

Key Features

- Freestanding and relatively independent of the urban structure surrounding it
- Tends to have one dominant side with reduced activation of remaining sides
- The transition and visible hierarchy between public/private is realised at the larger scale of the urban street network as opposed to taking place within the bounds of the block
- Responsibility for shared space surrounding the building(s) can be unclear

Design Challenges

- Designing landscaping of spaces around/between buildings and ensuring clarity of responsibility for their maintenance
- Design resolution of fronts and backs in terms of privacy, access and servicing
- Compensating for potential loss of street life

the built environment. These often have windows overlooking the street and can have multiple entrances giving access from different sides of the block. These civic buildings are usually of relatively high quality, with good care and attention paid to their detailing, and a decent budget to provide attractive and resilient materials. For these reasons, they have traditionally presented a very positive offering to the streetscape, although this has been borne out of their function and status rather than the affordances of this configuration, which is quite restrictive in design terms.

More critical issues began to arise with the typology when it was adopted by the modern movement in architecture as a solution to mass housing in the aftermath of World War II. Blocks of high-rise flats effectively inverted the traditional relationship of home to garden by sitting the block in an open space. It is at this end of the solitaire spectrum – where expansive distances are generated between the building's edges and the street network – that this block type departs from its former role as custodian of civic values. The urban terrains characterised by these modernist point blocks have been severely criticised in the decades since they were trialled, for the often wind-blown and ambiguous spaces between buildings that they engendered.

2.22 Example of a contemporary apartment building in a point block form, UK.

2.23 Example of a traditional 'solitaire' point block, Helsinki, Finland.

D – THE RIBBON BLOCK

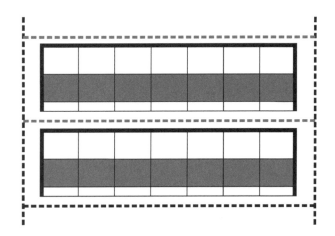

2.24 Ribbon block (diagram).

Key Features

- Discrete rows of accommodation arranged across the block facing in the same direction
- Just one side of the block addresses the street
- Single orientation simplifies planning for controlled solar gain

Design Challenges

- Activating the street
- Impact of car parking
- Ameliorating potential conflict between fronts and backs of adjacent rows
- Designing the interface between backs and the public realm

The ribbon block might be considered to be a version of the row block but they are fundamentally different in that all of the accommodation faces in the same direction (see Figure 2.24). This sets up a configuration that essentially divides the block into horizontal strips, with semi-private streets/passageways arranged across the block, allowing access to the front doors along each row, as well as the rear gardens of the rows opposite. The fronts of each row then overlook the rear of the row in front. The pattern can continue ad infinitum but is usually intercepted by vehicular transit routes that visually define the settlements into block areas.

This type offers very little of benefit to the urban network. In a standard square block with four edges, the pattern allows only one set of animated front façades, two blank gabled façades to the sides of the ribbons, and one set of rear façades. From a passer-by's point of view, the entrances all occur 'buried' within the block, and this type does not therefore lend itself to a wide variety of uses, being mainly adopted for terraced housing or apartment complexes.

On a positive note, although only overlooked on one side, the semi-private access streets have a good sense of privacy and can benefit from their own sense of identity and the sense of community this engenders, although careful consideration of the set-back of the front façades (i.e. front garden length) is critical to maintain a sense of overlooking of these passages. Maintaining a common orientation can also help the internal planning of the properties in relation to sun-paths, and the type also benefits from offering a largely non-hierarchical arrangement, depending on the surrounding traffic loads.

2.25 Example of ribbon block layout in Paderborn, Germany.

E – THE COURTYARD BLOCK

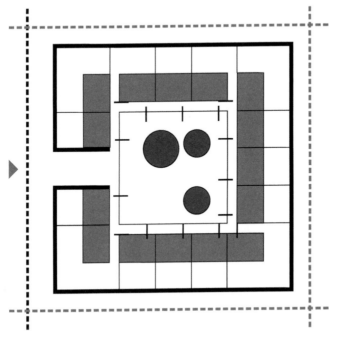

2.26 Closed courtyard block (diagram).

Key Features

- Inward-looking form with public fronts facing a central courtyard, where main entrances are located, while backs of units face onto access roads
- Good for engendering a 'collegiate' sense of community within the block
- Associated with discredited 'Radburn-style' layouts

Design Challenges

- Arranging the accommodation to activate the surrounding access roads
- Ensuring the 'back' façades presented to the road network are attractive, safe, overlooked and of high quality
- Ensuring the design enables clear distinctions to be made between public, semi-public and private realms within the courtyard enclosure

The courtyard block is essentially the inverse of the perimeter block. In terms of its urban configuration and massing, it is ostensibly the same, and therefore lends itself well to a permeable/gridded urban pattern. Yet the courtyard type differs fundamentally from a perimeter block from both a practical and a social perspective because its entrances and primary façades are located on the interior of the block. The urban cloister is a historically important version of a courtyard block, well known from monasteries and Oxbridge colleges.

The definition of a 'pure' courtyard block is largely determined by the following factors: that access to the buildings is not on the street network, that the inner core of the block is a semi-private space occupied by gardens or parking, that there is no prescribed vehicular route within it (although there may be access), and that there is a road or street network present around the outer perimeter of the block faced by the rear façades of the buildings and/or their gardens (see Figure 2.26). These distinctions are important because this type sits on a spectrum of inward-facing variants between the 'cul-de-sac' and the 'court' or 'close', as described in the section that follows.

The attractiveness of the courtyard block lies in its ability to foster a sense of community among its inhabitants. The clear physical distinction and separation from neighbouring blocks and the street network gives the inhabitants their own distinctive sense of identity and belonging – this is an important feature of this

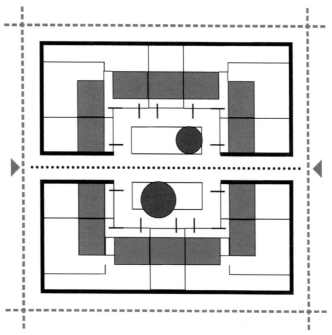

2.27 Open courtyard block (diagram).

block type that was historically used by Oxbridge colleges to foster a collegiate atmosphere of loyalty among their resident population of students.

The clear outlook of the comings and goings of inhabitants around the courtyard activates its inner core and encourages informal meetings and social interactions to occur within it. Meanwhile the windows of primary façades act as custodians of visibility to the inner core, meaning this semi-private space is generally felt by inhabitants and visitors to be overlooked and therefore 'safe'. The psychological influence of the courtyard block form on the creation of a community is incredibly powerful, and therefore harbours great social potential in design terms.

The corollary of its community binding qualities is the polarisation of activity away from the street, which is intrinsic to the courtyard block, and fundamentally problematic for the creation of an active urban network. The courtyard block effectively turns its back on the street, which engenders a consequent sense of indifference or even apathy to the wider neighbourhood beyond. The strength of the courtyard block is therefore its weakness in an urban sense. Careful design can go some way to overcoming these issues, and the courtyard block still has some mileage in urban terms if its pure form is disrupted.

Much about good courtyard block design can be learned from Oxbridge colleges. These are known for their grand entrances, which are often highly ornate and offer tantalising glimpses through to the serene and green enclosures within. The high quality and stature of the design of these entrances makes a significant outward-facing offering on one edge of the block, and naturally imbues a sense of identity to the adjacent thoroughfare. The inner-city colleges often lack a set-back and directly edge the street, offering a strong sense of enclosure and overlooking enabled by their high level of inhabitation, often addressing both inner and outer edges of the block at once. Careful attention to the detailed design of entrances offering visibility of the block interiors, appropriate identification of a mix of uses and consideration of the internal layouts of the accommodation, can all impact on how successfully the courtyard block operates in urban terms.

If the courtyard block is hybridised, then some of its negative characteristics can be ameliorated. For instance, if single-aspect accommodation is placed back-to-back in the manner of the Oxbridge colleges described above, then the negative consequences of the inactive outer façades can be overcome. This move naturally results in a much thicker and deeper urban mass, and consequently increases the scale of the urban grain reducing overall network permeability, but does allow the positive aspects of the courtyard to be enjoyed as one component of an urban smorgasbord. In this configuration, the courtyard is more akin to a 'close' typology, as seen at Hampstead Garden Suburb, or if undertaken at a larger scale, a 'square'. Alternatively, including a secondary route – probably pedestrian or cycle only – across the courtyard (see Figure 2.27), facilitates a higher level urban permeability, offering a secondary hierarchy of movement for slower traffic. The courtyard in this instance slightly loses its cloister-like character, but the urban flâneur benefits from being able to wind their way through such courtyard environments. Though these routes may detract still further from use of the outer streets, they still represent a significant urban offering for the user and maintain high levels of permeability.

2.28 A typical residential courtyard block showing blank fencing facing the street on the left-hand side, UK.

2.29 Aerial view of an open courtyard block, Dundanion Court, Cork, Ireland.

F – OTHER VARIANTS OF URBAN FORM

Despite the fact they're not block types per se, the following three variants of urban form are an important subset of urban block design. The court, the close and the cul-de-sac could all be defined as derivatives of an 'inlet' set, as inward-facing entities within a larger block type defined by a street network. It is important to differentiate these variants from the courtyard block, which although similar in its inward-facing nature, is fundamentally different in that it operates as a stand-alone block and is generally circumnavigable (although not necessarily accessible) around its full outer perimeter. Although the three variants defined here are similar in their inward-looking configuration, they have different origins, and the minor variations between them make for different relationships to both the street or space they front, and to the larger urban network that they stem from.

2.30 Example of a modern court type development at Ilchester Road, London, by Peter Barber Architects.

F1 – THE COURT

Key Features

- Typically configured as 'inlets' facilitating densification/subdivision of larger plots
- Potential to foster a 'collegiate' community spirit
- Historically associated with overcrowded slums but being reinvented as urban enclaves suited to small dwellings meeting modern standards and expectations

Design Challenges

- Providing for car parking without spoiling the quality of open space
- Ensuring privacy for occupants of facing units

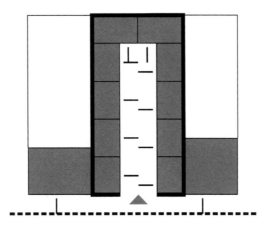

2.31 Court (diagram).

The court is a small, narrow and densely populated inlet within a larger urban block. It is usually comprised of a dead-end access lined by a number of individual plots (see Figure 2.31). The court is similar to the close in that it sits within a larger urban block, but is dissimilar in its scale and visual relationship with the street network, often being narrow with no – or limited – vehicular access, and with limited provision for communal amenity space beyond the common access way.

In its original form the court manifested itself through the intensification of the medieval burgage plot. These plots were occupied by a range of trades, and gradually subdivided and built up to enclose new streets. The street building (burgage tenement) emerged as the staple building block of the medieval street. Saving space, the plot was usually developed up to its front boundary, providing a direct interface with the street, while the rear overlooked private gardens and courtyards. Where towns and cities became overpopulated, however, the relatively generous proportions of burgage plots led to subdivision into smaller and smaller plots, and in some cases to 'courts', where the plot boundary was lined with small single-aspect dwellings facing inwards.

In the 19th century, the slum conditions of courts discredited them and led, ultimately, to their wholesale demolition in favour of row blocks. In more recent times there is evidence that housing shortages, combined with the desire to make more efficient use of urban land, may be stimulating a renaissance of the court typology, still single-aspect, but with more desirable living conditions.

F2 – THE CLOSE

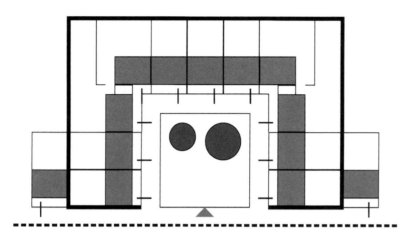

2.32 Close (diagram).

The close is an innovation of garden city design, manifesting as a generously proportioned inlet to the larger block. The increased length of the overall perimeter of a large block offered a more intimate shared space to a cluster of dwellings recessed from the street. The close itself is usually three-sided, and of similar width to length, with one edge of the semi-enclosure defined by its edges remaining open to the street network (see Figure 2.32). This offers significant advantages over the courtyard block and the cul-de-sac, in that it remains visually connected with the street.

The close offers the inward-facing characteristic of the courtyard block but differs in that the rear of the accommodation is set back-to-back against other accommodation, as if it were 'nested' within a larger perimeter block on a gridded street network. The 'nested' square/close resolves one of the main difficulties with the courtyard block, which is how its rear façades relate to the street network, and means that the urban locality still benefits from a permeable urban structure edged by fronts of buildings around its full perimeter.

Achieving a close is contingent on being nested within a wider urban structure. By definition, only a limited proportion of accommodation can be located within such an inlet: an urban network consisting entirely of abutting squares/closes is not possible to achieve without culminating in a tree-like branched network, which – brought to its logical conclusion in the form of the cul-de-sac – sits uncomfortably in the designer's repertoire of urban forms. The close is therefore inherently hierarchical due to its social and economic relationship to both the block it nests within and to the wider street network.

Key Features

- Typically configured as 'inlets' enclosing a shared space within larger or irregularly shaped urban blocks, enabling denser inhabitation and more efficient use of land
- Often with an open relationship to the street
- Potential to foster a 'collegiate' community spirit

Design Challenges

- Moderating the hierarchy between the units within the relative enclosure of the close against their outward-facing neighbours set around the host urban block
- Providing car parking without spoiling the quality of the communal open space
- Landscaping the open space and ensuring clarity of responsibility for its maintenance and upkeep

2.33 Aerial view of a close set within a suburban perimeter block of semi-detached houses. This example highlights the blurring of boundaries between the 'close' and the 'cul-de-sac' in suburban developments that followed after the garden city movement.

F3 – THE CUL-DE-SAC

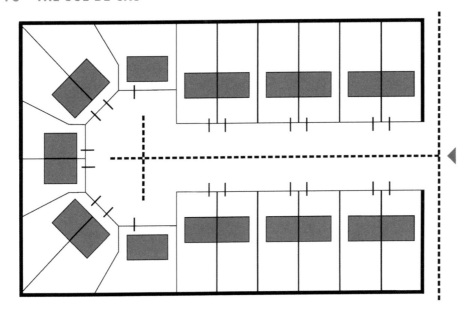

2.34 Cul-de-sac (dead end) (diagram).

The cul-de-sac is a group of dwellings or buildings grouped around a dead-end street (see Figure 2.34). The configuration differs from the courtyard block or close in that it usually substitutes communal space for access. Similar to the court, it is usually two-sided with one closed end. But whereas the court is essentially an urban phenomenon – an infilling of what originated as a single burgage plot – the cul-de-sac is a suburban one. Unfettered by pre-existing plot boundaries, it usually manifests itself as being much longer than the court or close, with lower-density houses.

Although often enjoyed by residents due to their intimate feel and sense of defensible space, the wholesale adoption of the cul-de-sac as a model for suburban development thus creates a dendritic pattern of development that strangles permeability. In an urban network designed specifically for the cul-de-sac, swathes of cul-de-sacs can be located adjacent to one another, meaning that the proportion of accommodation essentially 'benefitting' from an inward-facing outlook is infinitely higher than the 'close' or 'court' variants are able to offer. This goes some way to explain their phenomenal success as the typology of choice for UK house-builders, but wholesale adoption of this type offers a bleak outlook for maintaining the role of the street, and the complexity and conviviality of urban life associated with it.

Key Features

- An inlet within a (typically) suburban block, comprised of vehicular access with a dead end surrounded by buildings, usually dwellings

- Can sometimes foster a similar 'collegiate' community spirit as a courtyard block, although low-density models without a central or common open space are less likely to stimulate social interaction

- Associated with low levels of permeability and consequently higher dependence on car transport than traditional block types

Design Challenges

- Providing space for social interaction to occur for community cohesion while ensuring clarity of responsibility for the maintenance and upkeep of such spaces

- Awareness of the implications of car reliance this model necessitates and including initiatives to counteract this, such as limiting the length of the cul-de-sac and providing for pedestrian and cycle connectivity between adjacent cul-de-sacs

2.35 A group of three typical cul-de-sacs with semi-detached housing.

SUMMARY

This chapter has established a taxonomy of commonly used block types and related urban forms, ranging from public/outward-facing (the perimeter block) at one end of the spectrum, through to exclusive/inward-facing (the courtyard block and cul-de-sac) at the other. The related urban forms can either occur as elements that are inserted within urban blocks, or they can negate the block altogether. The case examples that follow will be analysed with reference to the core types defined in this chapter, however as will be made clear, some examples are hybrids, and as such incorporate characteristics of more than one type. It is this potential for adaptation and innovation of the block that confirms both the continued relevance of the perimeter block to urban designers and the role that hybrid forms can play in enriching the urban experience.

3

DESIGNING
THE BLOCK

This chapter sets out the key principles of urban block design. The first section (Structuring the Block) gives an overview of the broader parameters and guidelines informing good block design, from urban structure (the network) and block size and shape, through to street-block hierarchy, density and grain, and social mix. Following this, the section on Design Principles provides greater detail on both the quantitative and qualitative features of block design, and how they interrelate or occasionally conflict. This is followed by a discussion about designing corners and parking, both of which have important roles to play in achieving successful block configurations.

STRUCTURING THE BLOCK

Any form of design practice involves multi-stranded thinking, and urban design practice also requires an awareness and application of multiple scales and aspects of the built environment to be woven into a complex yet harmonious entity. These have been notionally separated into three broad strands of design thinking, operating firstly at the level of two dimensions (the urban structure or network); secondly at the level of three dimensions (massing); and thirdly at the level of four dimensions (use and occupation over time). This tripartite model provides a helpful tool for conceptualising the multifaceted nature of urban design across its full spectrum of scale, from the city through to the block and plots within it. These sections also broadly align with the advice, experience and intelligence offered by influential theorists and practitioners that we reference together with urban design guidance documents that have been produced in the recent past.

URBAN STRUCTURE (TWO DIMENSIONS: PLAN)

PERMEABILITY

Permeability refers to the degree to which an urban (or suburban) area offers choice of through movement. As such it is not an 'absolute', and the degree to which any given area is permeable (and indeed the extent to which permeability is desirable) may vary widely. In general terms, cul-de-sacs (dead ends) by definition are impermeable forms of development, compared to layouts with small blocks that are interconnected by streets or other kinds of routes.

There is already a consensus that permeability lies at the heart of healthy urbanism. Design at the level of the block therefore presupposes design at the wider level of the street and block together conceived as a lattice, configured to accommodate a range of movement hierarchies and neighbourhood functions operating at different scales. In this way streets and blocks both inform and are informed by one another to produce urban structure. How that structure is configured then determines how permeable it can be. Campbell[1] advocates a reimagining of the discredited model of the neighbourhood as an isolated cell inherited from Clarence Stein, Perry and others, as an assemblage of blocks nested within a permeable superblock. For him, the superblock is a collection of multiple urban blocks, street blocks, open spaces and other uses bounded by city-scale streets or arterial routes rather than by local streets.

The block itself is an assemblage of parts and need not be seen as an impermeable unit of urban form in itself. The mews block, for instance, will often allow movement through its central access street, which effectively halves the size of the block in terms of its permeability for pedestrians. This is referred to as 'filtered permeability', where a denser network is available for lower-order traffic, allowing pedestrian and cycle movement to flourish.

Permeable superblocks already exist in some planned cities (notably Edinburgh New Town and Savannah, Georgia) and their success as urban places is testament to the robustness of the model. This model is also the default setting for some seemingly unplanned cities such as Tokyo (see Figure 3.1), where high population densities coupled with limited space have produced a pattern of 'superblocks' comprising an almost labyrinthine network of shared-surface streets and alleys that are both pedestrian- and cycle-friendly, lassoed by more heavily trafficked streets.

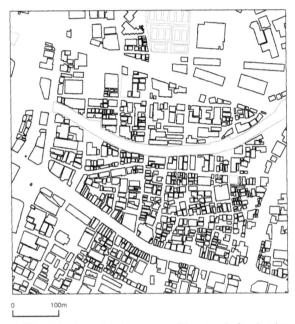

0   100m

3.1 The Tokyo 'superblock' – a permeable network of pedestrian-friendly streets surrounded by higher-order streets.

Cul-de-sac layouts do not support the articulation of perimeter blocks into land parcels, as they actively restrict vehicular and pedestrian permeability. As Bentley et al. argue, however, 'This is not to say cul-de-sacs are *always* negative: they support responsiveness if they offer a choice which would otherwise be missing. But they must be added to a permeable layout, not *substituted* for it.'[2] Similarly Campbell argues that the street network must at least have the qualities of openness and adaptiveness, because these qualities '...are essential for fostering complexity and structuring complex choices'.[3]

Figure 3.2 illustrates the relationship between permeability and different types of urban structure in diagrammatic form: 'gridded' or 'webbed' street networks are naturally more permeable than dendritic patterns, allowing clear public accessibility around the network, as well as defining the perimeter edges of urban blocks. These patterns are typified in origin by a network of straight streets intersecting at right angles, while the 'organic grid' is a less orderly version of a grid that might incorporate blocks with more or fewer edges, non-aligned crossroads, and curved or angled streets that have been distorted for one reason or another.

Radial and web patterns meanwhile offer the same qualities of permeability and adaptability but are planned in order to create and facilitate a central focus. Their grid layout morphs in order to direct arterial streets toward a common centre, with a corresponding graduating hierarchy of block types radiating from this, declining in their density, while increasing in scale toward the outer perimeter.

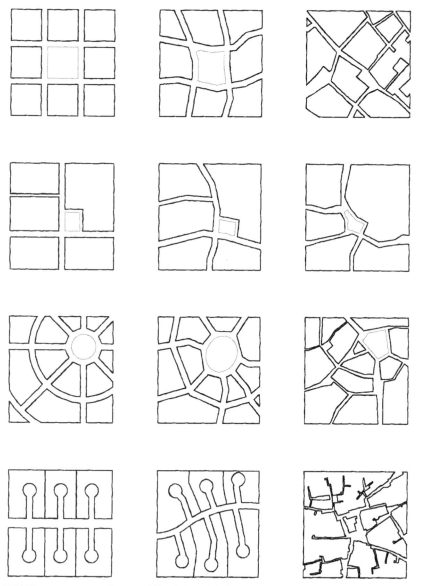

3.2 Urban structure and permeability. Left to right from top: **highly permeable (small blocks):** orthogonal grid; warped grid; 'organic grid'; **medium permeability (mid–large blocks):** orthogonal grid; warped grid; 'organic grid'; **varied permeability (small–large blocks):** radial grid; warped radial grid; 'organic radial'; **impermeable (large blocks with dead ends):** orthogonal cul-de-sacs; warped cul-de-sacs; 'organic cul-de-sacs'.

Dovey[4] notes that often the most obvious measures of permeability based on average block size (length, area, perimeter) can be misleading and suggests an alternative measure developed by Pafka, called the 'area-weighted average perimeter', where each block perimeter is multiplied by its area and then averaged across a study area.

BLOCK SIZE AND SHAPE

There is no 'one size fits all' formula for determining the appropriate size of an urban block. Appropriateness is dependent on understanding the complex interplay of locational context (urban, suburban, rural), accessibility (transport links), land use (civic, workplace, mixed-use, residential, etc.) as well as regionally and/or culturally specific building typologies.

In a UK context, the smallest sensible perimeter block depth for single-family housing might be based on a depth ('thickness') of accommodation around the perimeter of 6–10m (providing dual aspect and good daylighting), and a 20m clear space within the block (generally accepted good practice for privacy), preferably with a zone of defensible space ringing the outer edge, so totalling a minimum block width of around 32–50m.

Figure 3.3 shows that the minimum width block produces a form not dissimilar to the Victorian row block (albeit the Victorian version was less likely to incorporate defensible space or back-to-back distances). It is also noteworthy that such a narrow depth of block does not readily allow space for housing along the short side of the block, without reducing frontage along the long side.

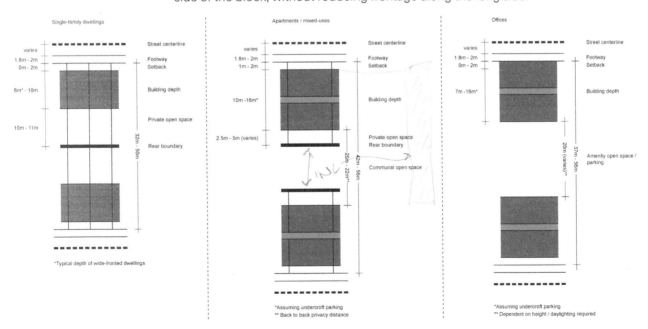

3.3 Minimum block depths.

Nevertheless the depth of the accommodation (increasing up to, say, 10–14m for naturally ventilated offices or apartments with double-loaded corridor access), clear space to the interior and an outer ring of defensible space can thus be increased (or decreased as appropriate) from this basic starting point, although adoption of smaller blocks should not be discounted where a design imperative takes precedence over accepted privacy sight-distances, for instance.[5] The depth of accommodation of both apartment and office buildings is often affected by parking considerations. For example, if parking is provided under the building footprint, a depth of around 16m (e.g. 2 × 5m long car parking bays separated by a 6m wide aisle) is needed.

If the appropriate depth of a block is thus a product of its context, as described above, determining the appropriate length of the block is similar to raising the question 'how long is a piece of string?' This is where permeability comes to the fore. Victorian developers often elongated row blocks to as much as 200m for the sake of economic efficiency, but at the expense of permeability.

Jane Jacobs defined her golden standard for walkable neighbourhoods as being a maximum of 100m in either direction, and this remains a good rule of thumb, with the caveat that square blocks are less efficient than oblong ones. Accordingly, the *Urban Design Compendium* suggests a slightly smaller grid spacing of 80–90m as a rule of thumb, although proposes this be decreased to 50–70m or 60–80m in central areas with intensive pedestrian activity. The *Compendium* illustrates a range of viable block sizes, from the smallest at approx. 15m × 15m to the largest at approx. 185m × 115m, advocating a variety of different block sizes as best practice for mixed-use neighbourhoods.[6] Dovey meanwhile suggests a maximum block area of 1 hectare as a good rule of thumb.[7]

Smaller block sizes offer less scope for overall density, due firstly to the increased area of roadways in proportion to development land and secondly to the fact that the cost and size of vertical circulation means it is less economical to build tall on a small site. These negatives have to be countered, however, by the fact that smaller block sizes allow the creation of walkable, flexible, diverse and (as a result) potentially more attractive neighbourhoods.

The footprint of a block depends on its use (commercial, leisure, residential, etc.), on the hierarchy of the street it fronts (primary, secondary, tertiary routes) and on the local context or topography. Rectangular blocks are useful for mixed-use blocks where the short end can be assigned a commercial or civic use on a busy route, with residential accommodation lining the longer sides. Square blocks are generally considered most flexible for a wide range of uses, but as noted above, are not the most efficient. Block shapes can be distorted in all kinds of ways, and generally contribute interest to the streetscape, although blocks that completely lose their fourth side in the skewing or dissecting process and become triangular can be notoriously difficult to plan.

DENSITY AND INTENSITY (THREE DIMENSIONS: MASSING)

MASSING

There are numerous push and pull factors determining the massing of block form. The initial focus of good design must be to mediate between these sometimes conflicting agendas, and to define a three-dimensional form that is the 'best fit' for the site in terms of its context and programme. On an incrementally phased or self-build development, these massing decisions will most likely be informed by parameter plans or a 'design code'. Where a whole block is assigned to one 'designer', the task is more straightforward, but it still involves negotiation with a variety of parties, including the client, neighbours and the planning department, yet may not necessarily yield the best outcomes. The logistical situation is therefore complex on many levels, but the primary physical considerations determining form and massing could be summarised as: the relationship of the block to the local context, the spatial proportions of adjacent streets/interior courtyards, and environmental factors such as solar orientation.

The use, occupation and scale of local context will determine many decisions as to physical form and massing. The orientation of the block will need to relate to the primary and secondary streets around it. Decisions about height will need be made with respect to the existing (and proposed) use and enjoyment of adjacent properties, and in order to capitalise on local assets such as a square or green space. The arrangement of higher and lower elements of the block will also need to take into consideration the heights of neighbouring properties, and any important views to retain across or from the site (e.g. heritage assets), as well as views for the enjoyment of future occupants (with the added property value this can bring). Careful studies of overshadowing and shelter from wind are also important, particularly in exposed situations and colder climates. Whyte's well-known 'Street Life' project studied the social use of squares and public spaces in the USA, and confirmed that shelter and sun/shade are critical factors in the occupation of such public 'rooms'.[8] Consequently the tracking of sunshine across an outside space is one of the primary determinants of its use, as well as moderating wind speed.

Massing must also be carefully considered with respect to the spatial proportions of the exterior spaces the block defines. The physical form of a block implicitly creates a set of urban spaces or 'rooms', both around it (the adjacent street network) and within it (courts or streets depending on its arrangement). Numerous studies have examined the proportions of urban spaces (height to width ratios, and the sense of enclosure and definition they offer) that are thought to make them attractive and successful as places.[9] The block designer must be aware that the physical mass of the block form itself – the figure – inevitably generates an 'urban space' around it – the ground – and that the success of this external realm is perhaps of even greater importance to the success of a place as a whole than the individual buildings that make it up. Paraphrasing Gehl,[10] the design of the block must prioritise 'life *between* buildings, because the other way around never works'.

Sustainability also plays an increasingly important role in the massing of blocks. Solar orientation can affect the environmental performance of buildings dramatically, while also affecting the quality of life of its occupants. Solar collectors can be utilised to best effect when thoughtfully incorporated into the block design to achieve the best possible return, while minimising visual clutter. Prevailing wind should be factored into the arrangement of form where possible, to enable effective natural ventilation to take place. The 'microclimate' generated by form can also be moderated by its landscape design, and the considered integration of physical form and landscape should be considered at the very earliest stages of design.

The case studies that follow this chapter each demonstrate a slightly different combination of the push and pull factors that have influenced their massing, and illustrate the fact that some degree of compromise between these factors is almost always necessary. Nevertheless, careful judgement needs to be used in playing one factor off against another to achieve a finely tuned and tempered urban environment.

DENSITY

Density tends to be regarded as a 'target' of design rather than as an 'outcome' of other factors such as accessibility, permeability, assemblage and proximity. But in lively and vibrant places that people enjoy being in and living in, density (and its more elusive partner, 'intensity') is more likely to emerge as a consequence of successful placemaking than being a determinant of it. Accordingly, there is no point in prioritising density as a sustainable 'thing' in itself, rather we need to consider density as just one factor to be considered among many.

The most representative measure of density is the number of people occupying a set area over a 24-hour period. This isn't easy to calculate, and the more usual 'measure' of density used by house-builders or developers is dwellings per hectare (dph). This figure gives a pretty limited sense of the density of actual occupation, given that dwelling sizes, types and their occupancy levels can fluctuate dramatically, and that more diverse and complex mixed-use schemes include a range of non-residential uses not factored into this measure.

Poor sanitation and hygiene associated with high-density development and overcrowding during the Industrial Revolution was the driving force behind the Garden City Movement and of suburbanisation generally, giving density a bad name. Following contemporary research showing how moderate- to high-density living can contribute to urban sustainability, however, achieving higher-density development has found its way back up the planning agenda. Higher density helps to promote walkable neighbourhoods and healthier lifestyles, makes local services more viable, supports better public transport, promotes diversity and social contact, makes more efficient use of land and resources and reduces development pressure elsewhere. Although supported by policy, high density isn't on every client's agenda, and the policy drive towards increased densities on brownfield sites, together with the increased development costs associated with these sites (and growing demand for urban living), has compounded the supply-led development of high-density apartment buildings in urban areas, while perpetuating the demand-led development for lower-density suburban housing developments.[11]

Density is achieved by two means. Firstly, by tightly packing accommodation, which can have either positive or negative outcomes for inhabitants depending on the circumstance and use. Secondly, by building 'vertically', which allows more floor area to be achieved as a proportion of the site's footprint, measured as floor area ratio (FAR). In terms of physical form, designing a densely packed plan can dovetail with broader urban objectives such as enlivening the streetscape with multiple entrances, reduced set-backs and a more direct relationship between buildings and the street.

In terms of building higher, there is an economic relationship between density and viability that has a significant impact on form. Close-grain plots cannot achieve comparable densities to medium or course-grain ones, owing to the simple economic expedient of having to justify the costs of building high (with lifts) by having a greater number of units per floor to share those costs.[12] Housing expert David Levitt[13] points out that in order to keep lift service charges to a reasonable level it is usually necessary to share the cost between at least ten dwellings, and preferably between 15 and 20. This creates a tension between the number of units sharing a core and the height of buildings enclosing the courtyard, which effectively limits the height of the block. As height increases, however, it becomes viable to provide lifts with fewer dwellings per core up to seven storeys, above which it is desirable to provide a second lift as back-up in case the first one fails. This is the rationale for high-rise or point blocks as a mass housing solution, albeit one that brings with it a host of downsides, and it means that it is relatively difficult to achieve an economical high-rise block form that offers high density in tandem with the kinds of building form (e.g. perimeter blocks) that allow dual-aspect frontage, cross-ventilation or multiple entrances, etc. Campbell points out that high-density towers are disproportionately low on families and that low-density suburbs are disproportionately high on families, resulting in unbalanced communities. For this reason, he argues we must rediscover the 'sweet spot' of urban density, ranging from two to six storeys in height and achieving a density range between 50 and 150 dwellings per hectare, with sufficient critical mass to make them sustainable, and with a range of building types to attract more balanced communities.[14]

MIX AND DIVERSITY (FOUR DIMENSIONS: USE AND FUNCTION)

MIX AND USE

The idea of segregating land uses is inextricably linked to the death of the traditional urban block in the post-war period. The pendulum of opinion has already swung in the opposite direction, with the widespread acknowledgement of mixed uses as 'a good thing' and a rehabilitation of the block as the preferred urban form (at least of urbanists). But the pendulum has not swung quite so far as to provide a mechanism for incorporating mixed uses easily within the same block (i.e. side by side), much less integrating mixed uses vertically within the same building or plot (i.e. on different levels). Perhaps this is why masterplanning practice continues to identify the block as a unit of development and land use, rather than as a unit of different things mixed together.

For our purposes, the mixing of uses has a variety of implications for the form and design of the block, which we explore in a little more detail in the following section. The difficulty comes when the design imperatives of different uses don't quite align with one another, and uses that might have coexisted in times past (for example due to a lack of regulation) can no longer share the same space without significant compromises being made.

In a sense this is the challenge for block design, for which we cannot propose a simple solution, but we argue the way forward lies in a rediscovery of the underlying structure of the traditional urban block as an assemblage of independent plots, each capable of articulating its own urban agenda, so to speak.

DIVERSITY AND INCREMENTALISM

Arguably the single greatest failing of urban design in the latter part of the 20th and early 21st centuries arises from its simultaneous acknowledgement of the contribution of the traditional urban block – with its fine grain of plots, mixed uses and diversity of buildings and styles – to the success of established places, with its failure to provide for these characteristics in new places. It is easy to blame urban design for these failings but urban design doesn't control the market, and it is no surprise that the few exceptions to this trajectory have occurred in places where the municipality has shown the will and had the means (especially the ownership or control of land) to enter into joint ventures with the private sector to buck the trend.

Diversity in successful places is manifested in different ways and at different scales.[15] Variety of building forms, architectural design and age of buildings, mixed housing types, sizes and tenures, and a mix and intensity of uses, are all features of older towns and cities (and hence of urban blocks) that we cherish, but the conditions that produced these places no longer hold sway. Urban design practice has instead focused its energy on more readily achievable but less rewarding outcomes such as accessibility and permeability of urban form and structure without its essential DNA: the plot.

DESIGN PRINCIPLES

The relationship between the block and the street is symbiotic: neither one has any meaning (or life) without the other. The block itself is a kind of ideogram: it does not exist merely as a two-dimensional figure/ground, but as the coming together of streets, plots, buildings with their occupants and the various activities they engage in. It is one part of the urban fabric and, through mediating between the public realm of the street and the private realm of the individual, supports the wider framework of urban life. Streets usually have blocks on both sides, of course, so we must also consider the proportions of the street insofar as it is 'enclosed' by the three-dimensional forms of the buildings that make up the block.

The inside–outside relationship between the block and street, i.e. the built edge or 'street wall', is especially significant to the success of a street because as people we are drawn to the edges of spaces in preference to their centre. This is because edges aid and abet the way we have evolved to move and look. As a strategy, this trait – known as thigmotaxis, or 'wall hugging' – provides us with an egocentric frame of reference that we can use to construct a mental map of our surroundings.[16] If the edge works, so will the space.

Perimeter blocks also have an inside edge to consider. There are nuanced relationships between the 'backs' of buildings making up the block, and the semi-public/semi-private spaces of rear gardens or communal areas making up the interior of the block. In this domain cultural issues surrounding privacy as well as physical issues such as sunlight, daylight, ventilation and wind must be coordinated and reconciled with the practical and logistical requirements influencing building height and so on.

Put another way, there are relationships between elements of the block and the street and the block and the courtyard that are 'syntactic' in nature. These syntactic relationships overlap with other parameters that are more clearly derived from metric relationships, meaning they are qualitative rather than quantitative in nature. The usefulness of this distinction arises from the fact that while metric relationships may change arbitrarily, syntactic ones are more enduring. Factors affecting the width of a building design may change overnight, for example, yet the distance people are prepared to walk between buildings is more resistant to change.

THE BLOCK AND THE STREET

The degree to which there is a relationship between the constituent parts of the block (its buildings, users and their activities) and the street is the single most important factor in determining the potential for the street to be activated. This premise is based on the observation by Jan Gehl (and others) that there is often a correlation between the scope for outdoor activities and frequency of interaction of neighbours.[17] But as Gehl points out, there is no basis for concluding that social relationships between neighbours will develop 'automatically', merely that design which is conducive to such interaction may encourage social relationships to develop.

However, this relationship is also a nuanced one – people expect to be able to regulate the degree to which their lives are 'on show', and to keep some activities more private than others. Conversely a shopkeeper will want to attract people into the shop in order to generate business. This calls into question how contact with the street is filtered according to the nature of the building's use and the cultural norms associated with those uses. We argue this depends on four interrelated factors: set-back distance, transparency, height and surveillance.

SET-BACK DISTANCE

The idea of 'defensible' space has been touched upon, and research indicates that homebuyers feel more secure if their house front is set back from the street.[18] This is one way of putting 'space' between the street and the building, and it is usually demarcated by some differentiation of the surface combined with some form of physical barrier such as a fence. In European culture this demarcation signals that the transitional space is controlled: it is visible to passers-by, but clearly not part of the public domain. While the provision of a front garden is felt to increase security and privacy, it is also regarded as increasing opportunities for neighbours and passers-by to interact, assuming there is an entrance to the house from the street. Of course, as pointed out by Levitt,[19] the front garden and how its boundary is treated also plays an important practical part, incorporating space for refuse and recycling bins and utility meters, etc. without necessarily obstructing the view out.

He goes on to suggest there is a fine line to be struck between adhering to the principle of active frontages by keeping visual contact open, while screening unkempt gardens from public view. This is the opposite side of the privacy coin, because passers-by may prefer not to be exposed to the private lives of others.

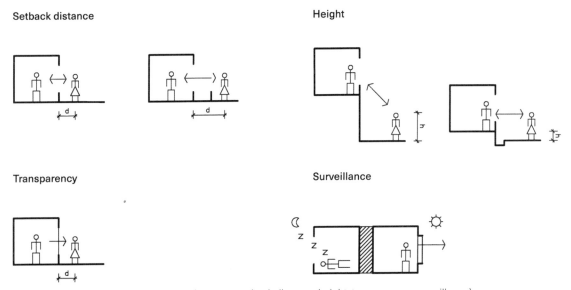

3.4 The block and the street (left to right from top: set-back distance; height; transparency; surveillance).

The distance between the house and the street is usually a function of land value and consequently, a measure of economic standing: traditional row housing has little or no set-back, whereas higher-value detached houses are more likely to have a generous front garden. In Georgian townhouse design, the separation of the house from the street was usually achieved by a lightwell – a void that allowed daylighting to the kitchens at lower ground level, and by raising the entry level a few steps above the street. In this way affluent residents could separate themselves from the street without the need for a large front garden. The lack of a private garden was instead compensated by the provision of a large communal garden to which only residents were given access.[20] Contemporary expectations demand equality of access for people with disabilities, however, so raising the threshold is not a simple design decision.

3.5 Urban row housing in Amsterdam with no set-back: these residents have colonised the footpath to create their own amenity space.

The closer the building threshold is to the street, the more readily interaction between the two can take place. Shops, cafés and restaurants typically front directly to the street with no set-back, and often 'spill out' with their wares or seating for customers. The closer together they are, the more entrances there are, and the more active the frontage will be. The same goes for housing, and the tighter the grain of buildings or plots, the more entrances can be provided to activate the street.

HEIGHT

Another way of putting distance between ourselves and the street is height. Perhaps for similar bio-evolutionary reasons as identified by Sussman and Hollander, we feel 'safer' sleeping above the level of the street. More subtle changes in level can be used to create a heightened sense of security but as mentioned above, these devices need to be reconciled with the need to maintain equal access for people with disabilities.

The level at which meaningful human contact with the ground is diminished or lost is perceptual, but Gehl argues: 'Between the third and fourth floors a marked decrease in the ability to have contact with the ground can be observed.'[21]

3.6 This residential development in Hammarby, Stockholm, uses a change in level to mediate between the public and private realm.

TRANSPARENCY

The next layer of control is the building envelope itself. As alluded to above, most dwellings are designed with a window to the street, but residents may seek to control the degree to which outsiders can see in. In traditional English and Irish culture, the 'front room' of a house is regarded as a kind of interstitial space between the public world of the street and domesticity. This is the room where visitors would be 'received', but it would be occasionally used by the residents themselves. Intervisibility between the front room and the street is traditionally controlled by net curtains that restrict views in while allowing views out. In European culture, however, the front room is regarded as a kind of statement: one doesn't use curtains unless one has something to hide. The Dutch take this a step further, regarding the front window as a kind of shop window: the 'place where one shows oneself'.[22]

3.7 Timber screens and a planted zone moderate transparency in this apartment housing in Arabia, Helsinki.

In contrast, Arabic culture prioritises familial privacy above all else and so traditional Arabic housing is impermeable to the street. Modern housing in the Middle East is still derived from courtyard forms and compounds, with careful control of views. Instead, 'street life' as we understand it in the West, is confined to bazaars, or in modern cities the covered shopping mall.

Designers therefore need to be sensitive to the cultural norms within which they are operating in order to resolve these issues, the Dutch and Middle Eastern expectations of privacy being examples from opposite ends of the spectrum.

But windows don't just put 'eyes on the street' in the sense of surveillance – at a deeper, subconscious level, windows are the eyes of the street. Sussman and Hollander[23] draw on findings from psychology and neuroscience to show how we identify with some places more favourably than others if, at a subconscious level, they recreate faces.

SURVEILLANCE

A recurring theme in urban design is the perceived benefit of overlooking the street. At one level, windows enliven the street scene and make it more attractive. More importantly, streets feel safer when they are overlooked because it deters antisocial activity. This is only likely to be effective if the rooms overlooking the street are 'habitable' in the sense that they are likely to be occupied and used. For this reason, it is preferable to position habitable rooms facing the street, with bedrooms and bathrooms to the rear. There are practical benefits to this arrangement because the inside of the block will be naturally more private, as well as being more conducive to sleep. Surveillance of the street can also be enhanced by bay windows, because they allow a wider angle of view.

THE BLOCK AND THE COURTYARD

Block size at the macro level is affected by numerous interrelated considerations such as the play-off between the costs and benefits of creating permeable and accessible movement networks. At the level of the individual block, internal dimensions are affected by further, more finely tuned considerations, of which building use, solar access and privacy are key. To complicate matters, solar access depends on the presence or absence of obstructions and so there is an interrelationship between block width and height.

BUILDING USE

In general terms the thickness of the block's perimeter is determined by the nature and intended use of the buildings surrounding the unbuilt interior or courtyard. Individual houses break down into wide-fronted and narrow-fronted forms. Wide-fronted houses are thinner, but less dense than narrow-fronted houses, which can be packed closer together. Apartments can be configured to be 'dual aspect' (i.e. having access to both the front and rear of the building), or as 'single aspect' (i.e. having access on one side only). Single-aspect blocks are occasionally configured to 'wrap' another type of building but more commonly take the form of arrangements with apartments accessed from a central corridor. This is more efficient than dual-aspect arrangements because higher densities can be achieved, however the dwelling units do not benefit from through ventilation, and only get the sun from one side.

As a rule of thumb, daylight will not penetrate more than 7m and through ventilation will not naturally occur beyond 14m. Because office uses also rely on daylight, these two figures taken together tend to result in building thicknesses of 6–7m for wide-fronted dwellings to 14m for buildings with double-loaded corridors, whether they are offices or apartments.

Daylighting will also be improved with taller windows and this, together with the depth needed to accommodate building services such as mechanical ventilation

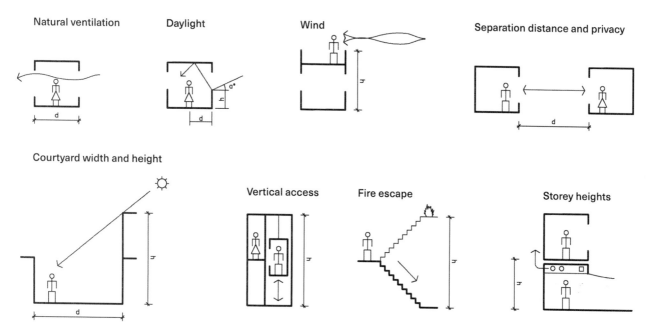

3.8 (Left to right from top) Block thickness and environmental considerations: natural ventilation; daylight and wind; separation distance and privacy. Courtyard width and height: solar access; vertical access (lifts); means of escape; storey heights.

and lighting, tend to increase floor-to-floor heights, with a cumulative effect on overall building heights.

Blocks with double-loaded corridors are usually configured with wide-fronted apartments on each side to make up for the lack of through ventilation and ensure adequate daylight penetrates into the back of each dwelling. Overall building thickness is usually increased compared to dual-aspect arrangements, but there is still a trade-off between building thickness and liveability. Moreover, single-aspect dwellings facing north will always be dreary. Consequently, this form of development is usually avoided on east–west arrangements whereas for dual-aspect dwellings, east–west alignments have the potential to maximise solar gain for photovoltaic panels, as well as adding value associated with the demand for south-facing rear gardens (at least in the northern hemisphere). There is also a tension between the desire to achieve optimum solar access by facing buildings in the same direction, and the desire to activate the street on all sides of the block, which is covered in the case examples.

SOLAR ACCESS AND HEIGHT
Solar access to the inside of the block is a critical consideration affecting the relationship of block height to block width (as opposed to building thickness), because this will determine the amount of sunlight received by the courtyard/rear gardens. In simple terms, the higher the block, the wider it needs to be in order to create a pleasant environment within the block. For this reason, it is usually

preferable to position higher buildings on the north side of the block, and/or create gaps between the buildings to allow solar penetration.

There are, of course, numerous other factors affecting block height, of which density is a recurring theme. As the height of buildings increases, metric factors influencing the height of blocks come into play. Above four storeys, for example, it is not considered reasonable to have to walk upstairs, and provision of a lift will usually be expected. Suffice to say for families with young children or people with disabilities, it is not practical to walk up so much as one or two steps with a pram, much less four storeys. Height also affects the need for alternative means

3.9 Example of a shared block courtyard, Dublin.

of escape in case of fire, however this is more a matter for building design than block design per se. Lastly, as height increases, the useability of outdoor spaces decreases due to wind speed.

PRIVACY
Privacy is a delicate subject. Proximity increases with density and the potential for conflict increases with it. The need for privacy, and one's perception of it, is both personal and cultural. In the UK a back-to-back separation distance between opposing windows of 20–22m is an accepted standard. The *Urban Design Compendium* suggests that a separation distance of 20m is a good rule of thumb, with reduced distances suitable for mews developments. Reduced distances are also commonly accepted where back windows face gables, or where windows are not directly opposing.

The 22m 'rule' is a legacy of the Tudor Walters report on housing for the working classes, published in 1918 in the wake of World War I, which subsequently found its way into development control standards.[24] The standard is thought to have emerged from the report's recommendation to provide a distance of 70 feet between facing windows of houses, on the basis that this would ensure adequate sunlight to dwellings (specifically one hour of sunlight to a ground south-facing window in London on the shortest day of the year). This was transmuted over the decades into a standard intended to provide adequate privacy between the facing windows of dwellings.

THE BLOCK AND THE BLOCK

Most streets are lined with buildings on both sides, and so the design of a block on one side of the street must be cognizant of the design of the block on the other side of the street. This fact engenders a feeling of being 'enclosed' by the street walls. As has been explained, we have evolved as humans with 'wall hugging' traits, and this sense of enclosure makes us feel secure. Enclosure is therefore a syntactic relationship between our perception of space, which in physical terms is a function of the degree to which the street wall is continuous, and its height to width ratio.

Street enclosure

1:1 ratio (mews)

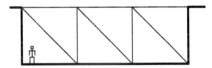

1:3 ratio (well enclosed street)

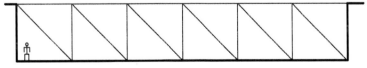

1:6 ratio (avenue or square)

3.10 Block height and street enclosure.

The *Urban Design Compendium*[25] suggests that a height to width ratio of 1:3 is generally effective (see Figure 3.10), with a suggested minimum of 1:1 for mews streets, and up to a maximum of 1:6 for squares or 'very wide streets'.

CORNERS

A recurring theme of urban block design (and especially perimeter block design) is turning the corner. By definition corners face two streets, and so offer the potential to provide more entrances to different parts of the building. Corners are also visually prominent and this, combined with their relatively high accessibility, provides both a challenge and an opportunity. The challenge is to design the corner of the block so that both frontages are activated, or at least overlook the street. The opportunity is available to include mixed uses in viable locations, or at least to 'celebrate' the corner, making it higher or distinguishing it in some way that bookends the coming together of two or more streets.

There is a range of strategies for turning the corner with apartment blocks (see Figure 3.11). An increase from two units per core per level up to eight or more raises issues to do with the affordability of service charges for lift access. A rule of thumb suggests at least 15 units are needed to make sharing the cost of a lift

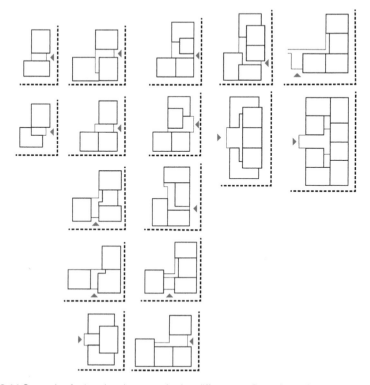

3.11 Strategies for 'turning the corner' using different configurations of apartments or mixed uses accessed from a shared core (not to scale).

viable.[26] Consequently, there is a trade-off between the viability of designs with fewer units per core – which provide more entrances but fewer people using them if no lift is provided because their height is then limited – and designs with more units per core, which are more efficient and potentially much denser, but with fewer entrances to the street, and higher numbers of single-aspect units.

PARKING

Parking is a contentious issue, and notoriously difficult to reconcile with the principles of good urban design in general and good block design in particular. This speaks to a tension between an individual's desire to own a car (or two or three) and to park it where they please, and the collective desire to create attractive and safe streets that are not car-dominated.

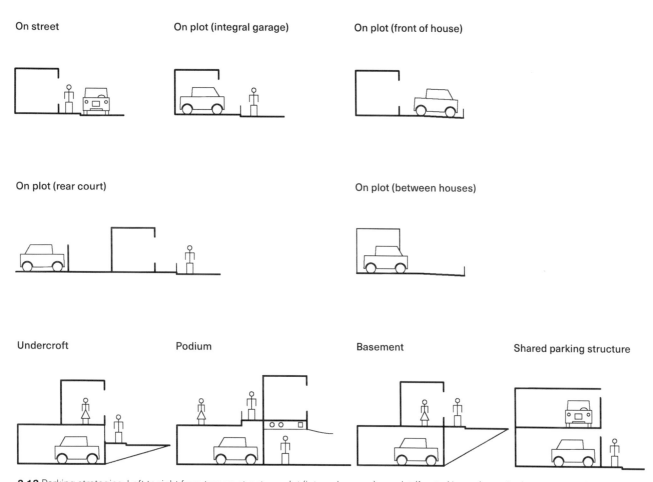

3.12 Parking strategies. Left to right from top: on-street; on-plot (integral garage); on-plot (front of house); on-plot (rear courtyard); on-plot (between houses); undercroft; podium; basement; shared parking structure.

Car-free developments have been mooted many times but, as will be explored in the case examples, even the most environmentally conscious schemes have had to contend with car parking in some shape or form. As illustrated in Figure 3.12, there are a variety of options to be considered, each with advantages and disadvantages, and each with implications for urban form.

ON-STREET

On-street parking is the default setting for many older towns and suburbs that were built either before cars or before widespread car ownership. There are many advantages. Like hot-desking, fewer spaces need to be provided because not everyone will need one at any given time. Most home-buyers and employers, however, value parking highly and this approach is not favoured in new developments. As noted by Levitt, there are practical and legal issues to contend with. Local authorities in the UK prefer not to take over the maintenance of on-street spaces and issues may also arise in the conveyancing of land to the house purchaser of a car parking space that is not part of the house plot they are buying. The presence of parking on the street is a mixed blessing. On the one hand, car drivers activate the street in their own small way and this human presence contributes to the use of the street. On the other hand, manoeuvring cars and traffic generally can dominate the street scene, making the street feel unsafe for children.

Nonetheless, the implications of on-street parking for urban form are fairly minimal: once parking is relegated to the street, the difficulties of providing for parking as part of the block design itself is largely avoided. There is an important caveat to this: square blocks use up more street with corners than long rectangular ones, meaning that longer blocks can provide more street parking than square ones, all other things being equal.

ON-PLOT (INTEGRAL GARAGE)

This option involves parking within a covered space or garage that has been constructed as part of the dwelling. Because most households tend to use their garages for storage rather than parking, however, this solution only works where the garage is provided in the form of a carport or covered space without a door; otherwise the car is more usually parked in front of the garage. In higher-density house types with narrow plots this form of parking is often provided effectively 'under' the dwelling, where the residents can't see it. Accordingly, to avoid potential security issues, it is recommended that this option should be avoided except in conjunction with house types that are wide enough to accommodate a front door and a habitable room at street level.

ON-PLOT (FRONT OF HOUSE)

Parking in front of the house is the preference of most residents, but most designers would argue that the set-back distance needed simultaneously weakens the sense of street enclosure and allows cars to dominate the streetscape. Parking on-plot is a sensible choice in some respects. Experience has taught us that if parking is provided out of sight of the dwelling it is less likely to be used and may result in parking inappropriately on the street or front garden in ways that have not been designed to accommodate it.

ON-PLOT (REAR COURTYARD)

Parking in rear courtyards seems an obvious solution but there are many pitfalls. If the courtyard is not overlooked it can become a magnet for antisocial activities and a potential route for would-be burglars or vandals. One answer is to gate the courtyard, but a more thoughtful response is to design the interior of the block as an inhabited space that includes parking, and is also overlooked by dwellings. This can help to make the parking area work, but still draws life from the street because residents arriving or leaving by car have no reason to use their front door.

ON-PLOT (BETWEEN HOUSES)

A favourite option of urban designers that is tolerated by both home-owners and developers is to accommodate parking between dwellings, behind the main building line. This combines the advantages of on-plot parking with reduced impact on the building set-back, but only works for detached or semi-detached house forms.

UNDERCROFT

Undercroft parking refers to parking under the block but at ground level. If the undercroft is not gated the parking area can feel insecure and will, in any case, fail to activate the street in any positive way. Undercroft parking is a useful strategy for areas at risk of flooding but does not achieve urban design objectives.

PODIUM

Many of the issues associated with undercroft parking can be ameliorated by this option, where parking is provided at ground level but under a shared courtyard space, with the ground floor parking screened from the street by active ground floor uses. This can work well if the ground floor uses do not need through ventilation or daylight penetration to the back, and so is suited to shops or cafés. This approach has been proposed for mixed-use blocks in the emerging self-build quarter of Homeruskquartier in Almere,[27] however there are few new-build urban extensions with the population threshold to support enough commercial uses to wrap a full block. Additionally, the podium level of the car park requires careful design for planting and ventilation to function as an amenity space as well.

BASEMENT

This is the most unobtrusive solution, but the cost associated with digging, tanking and ventilating an underground parking structure, particularly if more than one level is required, means it is only a realistic solution in central urban areas where values and numbers outweigh the cost. There are, of course, other potential pitfalls, including the lack of direct access to homes and potential security issues.

SHARED PARKING STRUCTURE

This option, entailing the provision of a separate shared multi-storey parking structure, is not encountered very often but it has been trialled in the eco-conscious Freiburg neighbourhood of Vauban, for example (see Figure 3.13).

Because environmental awareness is growing concurrently with improvements in electric car technology, however, the provision of car clubs using shared electric cars allocated to individual blocks could prove to be a gamechanger with the potential to bring this type of solution back into contention. On a practical level, of course, no one wants to carry their shopping any further than they absolutely have to, and so it is more likely to be provided in undercroft, podium or basement car parks.

3.13 Shared parking structure, Vauban, Freiburg, Germany.

ILLUSTRATING THE BLOCK

This book is concerned with urban form – substance – over style. To provide a useful reference point for designers, the selected case examples in this chapter focus on the strengths and weaknesses of the block's configuration in terms of what it contributes to the public domain, and how it fosters a sense of its own community.

The interplay of politics and economics that pertains to urban development sets the scene for any project's latitude before any design work has even been commissioned. The vested interests and motivations of the client, their perceptions of market demand and the interlocking cogs of planning and development processes largely determine the mix of accommodation the project will include, its quality, its phasing, and the scope and remit of any design work undertaken. The programme and land use of the block both affect, and are affected by, the development scenario, which often limits the physical testing of more daring and imaginative reappraisals of the perimeter block typology. The demand for housing in the UK has raised fundamental questions about delivery, and how to go about achieving a successful balance of public and private investment and control over housing and mixed-use developments.

The relative economic constraints of this present era have meant that there remain relatively few commissions by the kind of innovative clients or developers that would encourage the design of block configurations that stray from the financial surety of tried-and-tested models, and it is telling that the majority of the selected case studies are the result of progressive public sector involvement.

One of the most significant historical trends in the formation of urban blocks (and suburban blocks, albeit to a lesser extent) is that the prevailing mode of development has tended to eliminate the traditional subdivision of blocks into more or less independent building plots, and instead tends to treat the block as a unified entity consisting of a single plot, or a series of interdependent ones. There are few exceptions to this, and the consequence is that the majority of block developments are the product of a single designer. Despite this trend, the case studies cover a basic range of different approaches to 'designing' an urban block: from those that have been commissioned, planned and designed in detail by one 'hand', so to speak, through to those that have commissioned a plot-based masterplan where each plot is sold separately and built out on a first-come, first-served basis.

Given the complex history lying behind each block design, each case example includes a short commentary on the **project origins** and the development context of the block: how it came about, who owned the land, and how it was procured, so that the reader is able to comprehend the project in its wider socioeconomic context. There is detailed analysis of the **block configuration** in terms of its form, arrangement and relevant aspects of its detailed design, followed by a **commentary** on its successes and limitations, and its potential for replication in alternative socioeconomic contexts.

LIST OF CASE EXAMPLES

URBAN

Royal Road	Lambeth, London	2013	Panter Hudspith
Chobham Manor	Stratford, London	2018 ongoing	PRP and MAKE
BedZED	London	2003	Bill Dunster Architects
Barcode	Oslo	2007–18	Various/MVRDV
8 House	Ørestad, Copenhagen	2010	BIG

SUBURBAN

Poundbury	Dorset, UK	1993	Léon Krier
Kingshill	Kent, UK	2006 ongoing	Clague Architects
Abode	Great Kneighton, UK	2014	Proctor and Matthews

PERI-URBAN

Court Housing	Groningen, the Netherlands	2013	architecten|en|en
Neptune Logements	Dunkerque, France	2012	ANMA
Steigereiland	Ijberg, Amsterdam, the Netherlands	1997 ongoing	Various

'URBAN' CASE EXAMPLES

ROYAL ROAD

Medieval London re-envisioned

Location: *Southwark, London, UK*
Date of completion: *2013*
Urban context: *Urban infill*
Client: *Public (Southwark Borough Council partnered with housing association)*
Architect: *Panter Hudspith*
Area: *0.43 hectares*
Block dimensions: *60m × 68m (largest measurements)*
Number of dwellings: *96 duplexes and apartments*
Land use: *Housing only*
Tenure: *Mixed social rent and intermediate rent*
Parking: *Car-free project with cycle parking*

PROJECT ORIGINS

The London Borough of Southwark has pledged to build more than 10,000 new council homes over the next three decades and Royal Road is a pilot scheme for a series of new-build housing developments constructed by Southwark with 'development partners', titled 'Early Housing Sites'. These pocket developments will eventually go some way to replace the raft of council housing and land that has been sold off to private developers in previous decades, including the notorious demolition of the nearby Heygate Estate in 2011–14. Royal Road is the sixth of these Early Housing Sites, and arguably the best so far in terms of contextuality and quality.[1] The site is located just north of Kennington Park on the site of a former elderly care home, sitting beyond the official boundary of the Elephant and Castle regeneration district. It offers 76 new homes at social rent and 20 homes at intermediate (subsidised) rent.

The project has received a commendation at the MIPIM AR Future Projects Awards on the basis of its 'creative solutions in urban design, site planning and the human qualities of dwellings'. Southwark Planning Department also praised the scheme as 'an exemplar of high-density development'.[2]

BLOCK CONFIGURATION

This is a high-density social housing scheme in an unusual cruciform block arrangement (see Figure 4.1), with a strong community agenda. The cruciform configuration with set-backs

originated from the need to retain a number of existing trees on the site (see Figure 4.2). Although this breed of plan form may be criticised for the inefficiency of the length of its external envelope, the corollary of this is that reducing the *floor area : envelope* ratio increases the extent of available elevation – in this case enabling each dwelling to be double- or even triple-aspect, thus maximising natural light and natural ventilation.[3] The dwellings are of high quality for social housing in that they all exceed minimum space standards and that residents all have access to balconies, gardens and/or roof terraces. There are also no communal corridors here: all dwellings either have their own front door off the street or are accessed directly off landings within the four vertical cores.

The scheme is defined at its corners by T-shaped towers, each aligned with their respective street edges, jostling to assert their dominance of position within the somewhat jumbled plan form. Each 'T' contains a central vertical circulation core and one apartment is housed off this, within each of the three arms of the 'T'. Between these corner towers, along the two long sides of the site, are additional set-back blocks containing duplexes and penthouse apartments, bookended either side by the towers. These volumes remain visually distinct, connected at upper floors by mainly glazed walkways, but allowing passage through to the courtyard at ground floor level. The massing of this scheme therefore breaks up the volume of the block into six elements: the four corner towers and the two rows of set-back duplexes. Although the homogeneity of the materials and detailing gives the whole development an overall cohesiveness, these discrete volumes do offer their own distinct identities for residents within this. This is important because the surrounding streetscape, edged by post-war housing estates, lacks definition and identity, suffering from a surfeit of large scale blank gables and territorially ambiguous landscape.

The requirement for high density motivated the architects to draw upon medieval inspiration for the scheme, which ranges in height from four to nine storeys. The traditional fine grain of the medieval townscape inspired them to orchestrate a series of set-backs and staggered heights, which are used to give a different character to each elevation across the scheme (see Figure 4.3). This complex articulation of the massing helps to break down what could have been an overbearing scale and gives the impression of a more plot-based development. In addition, the architects pushed to try and ensure that each individual dwelling was unique; this was achieved by

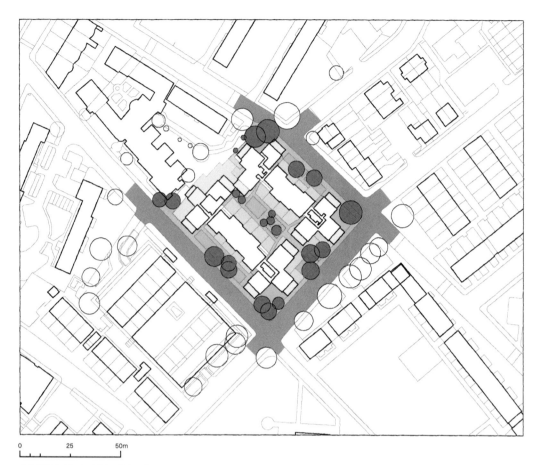

4.1 Block plan of Royal Road.

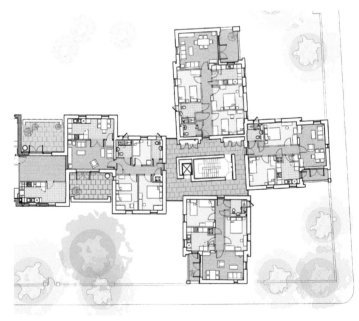

4.2 Typical upper level floor plan of Royal Road showing vertical circulation located at the centre of the 'T'/cruciform block.

applying localised tweaks to standardised dwelling types while safeguarding economic viability.[4] The broken-up massing combined with these individual tweaks results in an elevational variation across the scheme that offers a feast of visual articulation to the streetscape, achieved within its calming homogeneous framework of brickwork.

Chamfers are applied to corners at ground floor level, eroding sharp angles at entry points to blocks to create welcoming funnel-shaped passages to main cores. This effective tweak to the plan prevents the relatively deep entry passages from feeling pinched, opening wider views to public terrain and increasing passive surveillance from the street. In an ideal scenario, these four passages into the communal courtyard would have been openly accessible to the public, which would have granted the block an additional hierarchy of filtered

4.3 Exterior of Royal Road: (top) aerial view; (bottom) exterior view of block, highlighting the complex use of set-backs.

permeability, opening the central garden to non-residents and enhancing the pedestrian network. In reality this inner-city location required gates to be installed, and although the lightweight 'friendly' fencing offers some visual permeability, the courtyard remains for residents only.

Albeit private, the courtyard (see Figure 4.4) is nevertheless a successful space. The more constrained inner block proportions created by the cruciform and deep set-backs of the duplexes make the interior feel more intimate, while the largely vertical fenestration, generous balconies and terraces, and low fencing to the rear gardens of the duplexes, all palpably increase the sense of passive surveillance. The garden feels like somewhere you could safely send your kids to play while cooking dinner in one of the lower level apartments and is a reminder that bigger isn't always better when it comes to inner courts. Another positive aspect of the scheme detailing is the fenestration on both the street and the courtyard façades, which is predominantly full height, lending an elegance to the façades visually, while offering tantalising full-height glimpses into living quarters without over-exposure.

This unusual block configuration sets up a successful language of set-backs and hierarchies that allows residential high density to be achieved while maintaining privacy for residents. There is no mixed use included in the scheme and although this can't work everywhere, it does seem a lost opportunity for a development of this density. The ground floor elevations at the bases of the T-section towers – adjacent to the corner pocket-gardens – present an entirely blank face to the street, with high clerestory windows allowing limited light to the storage areas within; spaces that could potentially have been offered as live/work units, small office spaces or even a café to activate the street.

COMMENTARY

The additional level of complexity that the cruciform towers instil in their relationship to the street is the most interesting and unusual aspect of this scheme from the point of view of its urban form. They set up a block configuration that shouts out its potential for mixed use, but the necessary decision-making to achieve this would need to have been unlocked during the commissioning phase. Notwithstanding what could have been, this social housing block represents a triumph of planning and design, offering a wealth of spatial and formal devices, and learning from traditional plot-based development, that could be applied to other schemes.

Successes

- The block form enables a higher proportion of double-aspect apartments than is usually feasible.
- The crux of each 'T' operates as a natural focal point for vertical circulation, with the potential to foster interaction between residents.
- The form naturally creates semi-enclosed set-backs from the street that serve as defensible space for ground-level units.

Drawbacks

- The opportunity for the corner units to be activated by shops or other commercial uses has not been taken, and they are instead given over to bin and bike storage featuring relatively blank façades.
- The inner courtyard is not publicly accessible, denying the potential for filtered permeability the configuration is suggestive of.

[handwritten annotation] INDIVIDUAL UNIT DESIGNS CREATE VARIETY ACROSS THE FACADE WITHIN A COHESIVE LANGUAGE

4.4 Interior images of Royal Road: (top) internal courtyard; (bottom) view into courtyard showing intimacy of enclosure.

CHOBHAM MANOR

Something for everyone: a multi-faceted block of assorted London bricks

Location: *Queen Elizabeth Olympic Park, Stratford, London, UK*
Date of completion: *2018 (ongoing)*
Urban context: *Peri-urban new-build*
Client: *Public/private partnership (LLDC partnered with housing association and private developer)*
Architect: *PRP Architects*
Area: *0.68 hectares*
Block dimensions: *78m × 86m (largest measurements)*
Number of dwellings: *105 duplexes, maisonettes, apartments and townhouses*
Land use: *Housing with four retail/commercial units*
Tenure: *Mixed social rent and private freehold*
Parking: *Carports, podium parking and limited on-street parking for residents*

PROJECT ORIGINS

Chobham Manor is a distinctive and high-quality block-based development of family housing based on the edge of the Olympic Park in Stratford, London. The phased series of eight mixed-use blocks is in development at the time of writing. The multi-toned brick design theme has its roots in traditional Georgian town housing, but the scheme brings to bear a range of contemporary ideas about 'good practice' within an innovative block-based layout that incorporates a wide range of housing typologies.

Development of the site is under the auspices of the London Legacy Development Corporation (LLDC). LLDC's remit was to establish a new high-quality urban district and a strong residential community through their Legacy Communities Scheme (LCS). Chobham Manor will provide 859 new homes, 75% of which are family homes (three bedrooms or more), and 28% of which are 'affordable' homes offered through London and Quadrant Housing Trust (L&Q), with a mixed-use block including a café, nursery and flexible community space alongside apartments.

The masterplan uses the 'mews block' as its basis and defines a series of regular and irregular shaped and sized perimeter blocks of approx. 80m × 70m and ranging between three and eight storeys in height. The blocks sit within a permeable street network with a hierarchy of four 'grades' of route, ranging from 'major' avenues, through to residential secluded mews and laneways. Pedestrian access and choice are given high priority, offering relatively small block sizes of under 90m in length, which is effectively halved again once the filtered permeability offered by the laneways and mews is taken into account. The creation of sustainable communities lies at the heart of the design in terms of its social, economic and environmental credentials.

BLOCK CONFIGURATION

Phase 1A is a hybrid perimeter/mews block development (see block plan in Figure 4.5) comprised of 105 dwellings notionally organised into five 'parcels' of accommodation that utilise and integrate a variety of housing typologies and commercial or retail units on the corners at ground floor. The block perimeter is approximately 16m deep and comprises 93 apartments and maisonettes (five of which are designated 'affordable homes'), and a row of eight five-bedroom townhouses, clearly illustrated in the architect's 3D sketch diagram (Figure 4.6). The efficiencies afforded through vertically stacking duplex and maisonette units, allow frequent own-door entrances to be offered at ground floor level, which – combined with occasional commercial/retail units – help to activate the street. The ground floor elevations offer generously proportioned windows from the living accommodation, increasing passive surveillance, although cleverly set back within shallow reveals. A variety of planted buffer zones also carefully manage the thresholds between the block and the street and offer inhabitants the opportunity to contribute their personal identity to the visual patina of the neighbourhood as it beds in over time.

The design of corners has been carefully considered. The configuration utilises apartment units to undertake the task of turning three of the corners, while a unique 'multi-generational' unit including a rear annexe, successfully addresses the fourth corner. Set-back undercroft garden areas provided at ground floor level offer a soft and green treatment that ameliorate sharp street corners. Figure 4.7 shows the exterior of the Chobham Manor block.

The complexity of the overall block configuration is enhanced by inserting a row of four three-bedroom mews houses on a laneway bisecting the block. The façade of the perimeter block continues unbroken and the laneway is entered through a ground floor coach-style opening, albeit without gates. Although

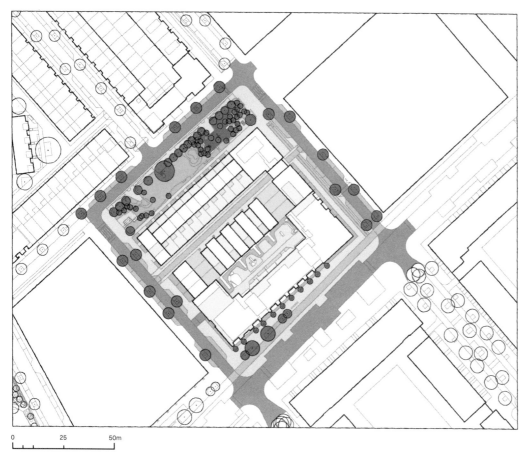

4.5 Block plan of Chobham Manor Phase 1a.

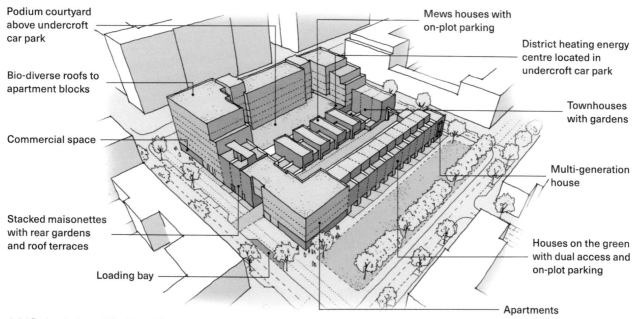

Podium courtyard above undercroft car park

Bio-diverse roofs to apartment blocks

Commercial space

Stacked maisonettes with rear gardens and roof terraces

Loading bay

Mews houses with on-plot parking

District heating energy centre located in undercroft car park

Townhouses with gardens

Multi-generation house

Houses on the green with dual access and on-plot parking

Apartments

4.6 3D sketch view of Chobham Manor block Phase 1a.

4.7 Exterior images of Chobham Manor: (top) townhouses; (bottom) multigenerational corner house.

the restricted access and sense of cloister-like quietness within imbues a sense of privacy, the laneway is nevertheless lifted from amenity status and treated with the same degree of care and high quality of finishes as the public block exterior, providing an attractive inner core for the surrounding residences to overlook. This laneway is not a standard mews configuration in that accommodation is arranged along one side only, and these dwellings face onto the undercroft parking of the apartments rather than rear gardens, so avail of internal courtyard gardens for their rear aspect and natural lighting. These four mews houses adopt a double-width front with carport to one side and a large picture window to the other side, providing overlooking of the mews laneway. While the carport gates opposite might otherwise afford this façade a service zone categorisation, the high quality of materials and extent of visible occupation means that the laneway feels safe and cared for. Figure 4.8 shows the interior of the Chobham Manor block.

4.8 Interior images of Chobham Manor: (top) mews houses; (bottom) mews laneway with coach-style opening to the street.

This block, and its almost identical sister alongside, are located on the south-east side of the 'garden avenue' that forms the community centrepiece of the overall scheme. In terms of the block's volumetric, the character and solar conditions of this public avenue are afforded priority over the block's interior. The arrangement of storey heights within this block therefore strays from good sustainable practice in terms of its orientation, in that the lower four-storey townhouses are located along 'garden avenue' to the north-west, while the higher seven-storey apartment blocks are located to the south-east, which does create some overshadowing with the block interior. This is ameliorated slightly by raising up the outdoor areas within the south side of the block to sit over the undercroft for this element, and through locating the semi-public and lower-rise mews lane houses to the northern end of the block interior, which doesn't suffer overshadowing. Although diverting from best sustainable practice, this composition of heights ensures that the overall scale of the neighbourhood remains 'human' and proportional to the street widths, and that the public avenue is more likely to attract activity and occupation – achieving a negotiated balance of environmental and social sustainability.

COMMENTARY

The configuration and details of the block design stem to a significant extent from the negotiation of public/private/shared/individual funding arrangements. Placing impetus on private developers to provide 'affordable homes' – as opposed to social housing being developed by the local authority – is the norm in the UK but is not without its critics. This scheme mixes freehold property owners with residents on part-ownership or social rent agreements, yet unusually the development agreement with LLDC stipulates that all residents be subject to service charges for neighbourhood management, thus allowing the environment and landscaping to be of higher quality than normally obtainable though local council tax funding alone. The block therefore benefits from use of high-quality landscaping materials that a council would not normally agree to upkeep.

The high level of thought and consideration that has gone into the design of the block is laudable, and this scheme represents an impressive showcase for 'good practice' in its carefully detailed relationship to the street, quality of materials, combination of dwelling types and mixed use, and its judiciously navigated social relationship to the merits of the wider masterplan.

Successes

- The wider range of house types than is usually found in a new-build block should attract a more balanced community (e.g. families, couples, singles and downsizers).
- The block's range of types enriches the streetscape and allows the scale of development to respond to the surrounding movement hierarchy.
- The relatively small scale of the blocks, combined with the mews configuration, facilitates a high degree of permeability through the area.

Drawbacks

- The fronts of dwellings on one side and the backs of dwellings on the other sets up a 'back-to-front' relationship.
- The innovative hybrid block type fits a lot into the moderate scale of its site, and the inclusion of the mews makes the overall configuration feel slightly over developed.
- The tight block dimensions compromise private open space making its interior feel somewhat squeezed.

BEDZED

Sun before street

Location: *Croydon, London, UK*
Date of completion: *2003*
Urban context: *Suburban infill*
Client: *Public partnership*
Architect: *ZedFactory (Bill Dunster Architects)*
Area: *0.57 hectares*
Block dimensions: *82m × 67m (largest measurements)*
Number of dwellings: *82 mixed-tenure duplexes, and apartments*
Land use: *Housing*
Tenure: *Public rent*
Parking: *Limited on-street parking*

PROJECT ORIGINS

BedZED is a flagship environmentally friendly, mixed-use housing development, with a distinctive visual character and strong community identity, located in south London. This experimental and slightly eccentric project emerged from an unusual form of collaboration between an architect (Bill Dunster, founder of ZedFactory), an environmental charity (Bioregional) and a housing association (the Peabody Trust). The project began in 1999 through partnering with Peabody to obtain a plot of undeveloped land earmarked for housing from Sutton Borough Council.

BedZED was completed to critical acclaim in 2003 and includes 82 homes, office space and Orchard College. The commercial success of the BedZED idea – and the marketable appeal of its quirky brightly coloured ventilation cowls – has propelled its property values to at least 10% above neighbouring premises of the same size.

BLOCK CONFIGURATION

The site takes the form of two adjacent 'blocks' containing row housing (see Figure 4.9). The southern, larger block is configured into three south-facing rows on a simple square block of approximately 70m × 70m, including a small inset courtyard on the north side. The northern, smaller block of approximately 45m × 45m has two rows of accommodation, including Orchard College and offices, giving the scheme its low level of mixed-use status.

The blocks are essentially a ribbon configuration in terms of their urban form (see Figure 4.9), with each row facing the rear of the row in front and narrow access lanes in-between accommodating the south-facing entrances to the dwellings. The ribbon elements are linked by a series of bridges at first floor level, which makes the combined set of rows read as a cohesive and homogeneous entity. The configuration operates as an urban block in that it could theoretically be continued ad infinitum on a grid network, although in this instance the development is ostensibly functioning as a cul-de-sac, given that vehicular traffic has just one access point off the adjacent main artery road, and this circulates around the two blocks of residences with no through route.

The project is a block design that has been oriented to the sun instead of to the street, which allows us to assess the implications of using sustainable orientation as a design driver in block configuration. Although its current incarnation is a set piece off a main road, the design also has the potential to operate well within a gridded urban network. BedZED also provides a relatively high number of dwellings per hectare, so provides a good suburban model for discussion.

The ribbon block configuration generates a hierarchical set of routes on the outer and inner block (although this is less relevant in this setting given the low volume of traffic on the encircling roadway). Ribbon blocks generally suffer from the one-sided nature of the inner access routes due to their relatively low volume of use, and from their largely blank side gables, but BedZED goes some way to address such concerns (see Figure 4.11): the fronts of the dwellings are oriented and designed for solar gain, offering high levels of transparency to the dwellings and increasing the sense of passive surveillance of the laneways over and above standard dwelling types. This façade treatment is augmented by careful consideration of the relationship between dwellings and laneways, where the depth of the gardens (varying between 5m and 10m between rows) and slightly raised ground levels (approx. 750mm) provide a happy medium between space for greenery and privacy for residents, and their overlooking of the access lanes through low transparent fencing.

The laneways are also provided with a sense of character, enclosure and a degree of activation from the almost arcadian planted bridges which span over them at first floor level, linking the horizontal rows of housing and providing north–south

0   25   50m

4.9 Block plan of BedZED.

4.10 Street view to front corner (south) of main block containing three terraces.

permeability to residents at this upper floor level (see Figure 4.12). It is these bridges that provide the most interesting aspect of the spatial configuration as they provide access from upper storey dwellings to their own private roof terraces sitting atop an adjacent block, establishing a north–south trajectory of usage in addition to the ground-level street running in the opposite direction. The side gables of the end row houses include entrance doors and small windows to increase overlooking, although these elevations still inevitably read as secondary. The fixed orientation and ribbon nature of this solar-oriented approach will always render its outward-facing qualities unidirectional to some extent, although the expansive fenestration, softened corners with occasional side entrances, and overall attention to materiality and detail, go a long way to address this.

Where a standard perimeter block configuration naturally encloses a shared collective amenity space at its centre, the ribbon block type doesn't, and to compensate for this, a small shared courtyard has been included at the northern end of the south block. This space is faced by the side gables of the adjacent rows and the rear elevation of the middle row, opening the interior of the block to the street towards the north. There are cycle racks and benches offered here, although the limited bikes stored here offer some indication of the perception of security. The question of how to incorporate shared amenity space in a ribbon block is always tricky, and the territorial uncertainty with respect to the collective ownership of this northern courtyard illustrates this point. The scheme does, however, include smaller pockets of clearly overlooked shared space within the laneways (albeit one-sided), which perhaps offer a more successful approach to this dilemma.

The scheme is a flagship because of its eco-credentials and as such offers a limited parking quota to encourage the use of local public transport. A small number of designated car parking spaces are located in bays adjacent to the flank walls of each row, with limited overlooking from the small side windows of the end residences.

COMMENTARY

Developing a block form that prioritises orientation to the sun over orientation to the street will always involve compromise. BedZED's design qualities ameliorate some of the negative aspects associated with ribbon block forms, although it perhaps remains questionable whether it goes far enough

to establish a 'model of good practice' for this block type. The project does, however, offer a positive contribution to consideration of future models of this type in the relative maturity of some of its spatial syntax design. More significantly, the project manages to effectively disrupt the rigidity of standard horizontal ribbon forms through its complex configuration of accommodation and unusual use of bridges, which generate an innovative woven three-dimensional matrix of circulation and inhabitation.

Successes

- The form facilitates repetition of house types.
- The front of every home is oriented towards the southerly sun, with generous although moderated provision for passive solar gain.
- There is a high degree of permeability within the block, at least in one direction (east–west).

Drawbacks

- Only one side of the block is activated in the manner of a traditional street.
- The lanes running through the block are quite narrow, making them overshadowed.
- The back-to-front configuration combined with raised front gardens results in a relatively low level of passive surveillance of the central laneways.
- The ribbon form of the block doesn't lend itself to the creation of a convivial shared space.

4.11 Exterior images of BedZED: (top) view towards internal street; (bottom) pedestrian street between blocks.

4.12 Interior images of BedZED: (top) within internal street with planted bridges overhead; (bottom) sky gardens linked to terraces by bridges.

BARCODE

Slicing up the mixed-use block – point blocks made good

Location: *Bjorvika, Oslo, Norway*
Date of completion: *2007–18*
Urban context: *Urban regeneration*
Client: *Public/private partnership*
Architect: *MVRDV, A-Lab and DARK*
Area: *3.53 hectares*
Block dimensions: *150m × 110m (largest measurements)*
Land use: *Housing*
Tenure: *Private*
Parking: *Basement*

PROJECT ORIGINS

Barcode is an experimental departure from the traditional perimeter block configuration that was originally earmarked for the regeneration of this former industrial zone on the edge of the city centre. The site sits prominently on the edge of the fjord near central Oslo, in which its towers are dramatically reflected.

The scheme design for Barcode was the successful outcome of a competition undertaken by the three collaborating practices. The competition guidance (prepared by the Norwegian government) requested three perimeter blocks, but the winning entry took an alternative approach, veering away from the brief in the hope they could win over the jury to a more creative and contextual solution. The team made a convincing case to shift away from the traditional perimeter block typology to open up framed views from the north side of the site towards the expanse of glittering fjord beyond, arguing that splitting up the site into strips would prevent the development from creating a high and impermeable wall that would separate the waterfront from the city behind.

The project was initially contentious with local residents – who campaigned strongly against the development – but the development consortium had both the power and confidence to see the process through to completion, and the scheme has since dramatically gained in popularity.

BLOCK CONFIGURATION

At first glance the basic configuration of Barcode appears as a series of eleven elongated 'point blocks', varying in size between 70m and 110m long by 5–21m wide, arranged as strips in a north–south direction and with a minimum distance of 12m between blocks. However, the form can also be read as a kind of 'super-block', combining some of the attributes of a perimeter block and a ribbon block. As with a perimeter block, all of the four sides of the super-block benefit from being frontages to some extent, with special design attention having been paid to the broken elevations to the north and south – where the short ends of the bars face the transport hub and fjord respectively – to ensure that these are not perceived as 'ends' and still provide welcoming street-facing elevations.

The eleven blocks are located on an overall development block measuring approx. 320m × 120m. This 'super-block' is then subtly subdivided into four smaller 'sub-blocks' by the insertion of north–south secondary access routes, one of which operates as a wide pedestrian plaza, while the other two allow vehicular traffic in the form of a more traditional access street. Each of these notional 'sub-blocks' then measure in the order of 100m × 100m and comprise either two or three of these elongated 'point blocks' with narrow pedestrian passageways around 9m wide separating them (see block plan in Figure 4.13). The shapes and heights of the blocks were sculpted with reference to their orientation and use and also to retain sight lines of the fjord from the higher neighbourhoods behind (see Figure 4.14).

The competition winning team drew up a masterplan and design code, setting loose but carefully contrived parameters for the design of individual buildings, which were then undertaken by a variety of different architects. The code offered a relatively high degree of freedom, providing a set of basic principles concerning form, volume, entrance and core locations, block heights, materials, programme mix and arrangement, parking and servicing of blocks, while still enabling design differentiation between the blocks. The development also took place on an incrementally phased basis spanning over a decade, beginning in 2005 with the PWC headquarters (A-LAB) at the west end, with the final block at the eastern end (also by A-LAB) being completed in 2016, all of which are visible in the completed development of 2018 (see Figure 4.15). This lengthy phased development demanded that a diverse programme with mixed uses occurred in each of the blocks. In the sense of its flexible

4.13 Block plan of western end of Barcode (initial phases).

0   25   50m

4.14 View of the completed Barcode development from the water.

4.15 Exterior images of Barcode: (top) 3D diagram showing evolution of Barcode form; (bottom) view of the rear elevations adjacent to the railway.

design framework, multiple individual designers and phased incremental construction, Barcode offers a healthy example of European post-modernist assemblage development.

The development differs significantly from a perimeter block in its increased overall permeability. Given that it doesn't provide a semi-private interior courtyard – similar to a ribbon block – the interior of the block benefits from a series of pedestrianised walkways. These external passages provide multiple entrances into the block and maximise the potential for publicly accessible commercial outlets, while offering some of the qualities of traditional townscapes such as Barcelona in their spatial proportions. The retail frontage is further increased by the inclusion of an east–west pedestrian route that cuts through the blocks at ground floor level, allowing sheltered access to additional outlets (see Figure 4.16). These routes differ critically from those in the archetypal housing ribbon block in that the overall scale and mix of Barcode allows the individual blocks to offer frontages on both sides, thus activating a double-sided, public-facing pedestrian network with a civic urban quality. In regard to its apparent permeability, however, it is important to note that the north–

4.16 Interior image of Barcode (view across access street).

south links are essentially private property, and not public 'streets' in the true sense of the word.

Along with its corporate occupiers, Barcode's convenient and attractive location also draws high-income domestic residents, making the significant cost of underground parking viable. It is this continuous underground service zone that is instrumental in enabling the streetscape above to be of high quality and remain free of parking, deliveries and rubbish collection. This splintered block therefore removes the hierarchies of public/private, outer/ inner relationships of traditional perimeter and ribbon blocks, offering a subtler and more publicly oriented hierarchy of navigable and accessible routes. The civic urban quality of these walkways will emerge over time, and their ultimate success will also be determined by surrounding localities yet to be developed as part of the Fjord City regeneration.

Meanwhile the gain in 'streetscape' (albeit privatised) is to some extent offset by the loss of the semi-public inner core that a conventional perimeter block offers. The communal amenity space in Barcode is relegated to rooftop gardens, and while these 'green tops' are visually attractive with expansive views, they lack the physical sense of enclosure, protection from wind and sense of overlooking that a courtyard scenario offers, with a likely reduction in usage, especially for families. The narrow inner streets of approximately 12m also set up short distances between facing windows, and views between blocks are uncomfortably close in some instances.

COMMENTARY

This unusual approach has taken strides to challenge the presumption in favour of perimeter block forms. Barcode is a high achiever in commercial stakes: maximising street frontage for commercial gain, enhancing pedestrian permeability of the urban network, and offering an efficiently serviced and high-quality streetscape. Its appeal to the domestic market is probably more limited, with the reduction in usable shared amenity space perhaps restricting appeal to high-achieving individuals and couples over families. The splintered form of Barcode was generated by the qualities of its specific location adjacent to the fjord and transport hub, its large scale, and its mix of predominantly commercial uses. Meanwhile its relative inhospitality to families, and reliance on high-revenue investment mean that potential for replication of this hybrid super-block layout remains limited to similar inner-city and highly accessible sites.

The success of this project is in spite of its urban form rather than because of it. As such, it is unlikely to challenge the orthodoxy of the perimeter block as the basic urban building block, with its clearer demarcation of public and private space, its diversity and flexibility. Rather, the relative triumph of the scheme as a 'block' can be attributed to the application of a strict design code that makes all the parts work together as a coherent whole, executed by a group of talented architects: simply lining up a row of point blocks is not what this scheme is, and is the reason we should not be seduced by its potential applicability as a formal solution that could work anywhere without the same degree of care and attention to design

quality. Urbanists claim that good architecture cannot save bad urban form, but the quality of this scheme – deploying point blocks rather than perimeter blocks – suggests this orthodoxy can be challenged.

Successes

- The allocation of each building to a different architect – regulated by an overarching design code – results in an attractively diverse yet coherent waterfront.
- High degree of permeability offering regular north–south streets between buildings, and a ground-level east–west passage across the whole site.
- The north–south breaks allow sunlight to penetrate through the block and facilitates glimpsed views of the harbour for residents to the north of the railway.

Drawbacks

- Privately owned north–south 'streets' between the blocks of accommodation enable a higher spec of finish and maintenance at the expense of freedom of access.
- The urban form does not provide for a shared open space within the interior of the block.

8 HOUSE

Streets in the sky with a twist

Location: *Ørestad, Copenhagen, Denmark*
Date of completion: *2010*
Urban context: *Urban extension, new suburb*
Client: *Largely private*
Architect: *Bjarke Ingels Group (BIG)*
Area: *2.1 hectares*
Block dimensions: *260m × 90m (largest measurements)*
Number of dwellings: *476 dwellings as row houses, duplexes and apartments*
Land use: *Housing, community, office and retail*
Tenure: *Private sale and rental*
Parking: *Limited spaces within adjacent multi-storey car park*

PROJECT ORIGINS

8 House is the largest private development ever undertaken in Denmark, commissioned in 2006 and completed in 2010. The private nature of the commission allowed the architect to be commissioned directly, while the progressive outlook of this largely commercial partnership recognised the marketing potential offered by 'big' design statements and provided a liberal budget to achieve this objective. The units here are on sale for around 25% above market rate for their floor area. The scheme has gained international recognition for its unique design qualities and was winner of the 2011 World Architecture Festival award for housing.

BLOCK CONFIGURATION

The architect, Bjarke Ingels, topically describes 8 House as 'a perimeter block that morphs into a knot' (see Figure 4.17). The cinched centre of the block defines internal courtyard spaces either side and provides a ground-level pedestrian access route across the block, which effectively slices the mega-block of around 260m × 90m into two halves of approximately 130m × 90m each. The predominantly vertically accessed accommodation (including a ramped street) maintains a consistently narrow front-to-back depth of 17m including balconies, allowing most units to be double-aspect with a range of orientations. The whole form is angled to maximise solar gain and scoops down from nine storeys at the northern end to just one at the south, resulting in some dramatic inclines.

8 House's high density and mix of uses enable it to operate as both a perimeter block and (to a lesser extent) as a courtyard block, with both inner courts and outer perimeter edges defined by a mix of residential and commercial units. The residential armature of the scheme recalls the well-known but discredited model of post-war mass housing euphemistically branded as 'streets in the sky' (or the less snappy 'streets in the air', as the Smithsons first posited).[5] Perhaps more closely related to seminal 'deck-access' perimeter block projects like Sprangen in Rotterdam than Park Hill in Sheffield, 8 House reimagines the simple deck-access approach into a complex looping helical ramp-cum-street, giving one-sided access to stepped 'row houses'. This unusual circulation route then operates as an additional 'stratum' of activity, making visible entrances to dwellings extending from ground level up to the tenth floor and traversing around both the inner and outer edges of the block. Bjarke Ingels describes how they 'stacked up the ingredients of an urban neighbourhood...into a three-dimensional neighbourhood where social life and ad hoc interactions normally restricted to ground level, occur throughout the building' (see Figure 4.18).[6]

The 1km looping ramped street is what makes 8 House special: its most distinctive feature yet also its most curious, impacting on both its inward- and outward-facing qualities. The establishment of a strong residential community is intended to hinge around informal interactions occurring on this ramped street, where social engagement might foster activation of the block's internal perimeter (see Figure 4.19). In addition, 500m² of communal social spaces for social, cultural and family events is available for residents, opening directly off the central crossover of the ramps.

In terms of social occupation, the simple act of ramping the access 'streets' critically alters the zoning and usability offered by standard flat 'deck access'. Whereas residents' personal occupation of flat deck areas is typically relatively informal and spills out across the circulation routes, at 8 House, the sloping nature of the access requires 'flattened out' areas to enable occupation, which in turn determines that the zoning between semi-public and semi-private is more clearly demarcated. The flattened areas then naturally become 'private' front gardens for the stepped row houses (see Figure 4.20). The ramp to garden dynamic remains very open, where the small change in level between each garden reduces the need for high fences, so boundaries are more subtly demarcated by

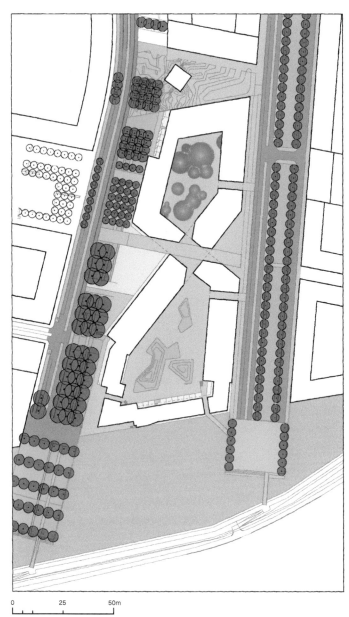

0   25   50m

4.17 Block plan of 8 House.

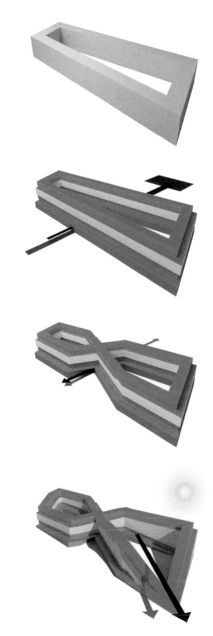

4.18 Diagram showing the evolution of 3D form for 8 House.

4.19 Exterior images of 8 House: (top) view towards south side of block from nature reserve; (bottom) entry point of ramped street.

shrubbery and steps. The occupation zones therefore sit on a spectrum somewhere between a typical 'front garden' and the informal occupation of a shared deck. The slope of the ramp is also relatively steep – exceeding UK building regulations for disabled access.

The act of raising routes off the ground plane immediately precludes free movement without a prescribed access route back down again. In this regard the scheme could be criticised for having created an elaborate cul-de-sac in terms of the ramps' accessibility, permeability and animation of the wider public realm. They are, however, more fairly compared to the standard deck access found in many apartment schemes, yet more thoughtfully designed and openly accessible. So for the high level of density achieved on this site, these ramps should more accurately be regarded as adding a welcome level of connectedness between the blocks' many residents and its visitors.

The ground plane of the block, meanwhile, is occupied by a variety of international and local businesses, including community facilities such as a nursery and a café/restaurant overlooking the water and nature reserve. The floor level of some of these functions is sunk a metre or two below ground level, which does limit their visual connectedness to the public terrain. Their access points are also quite difficult to fathom, as in some instances there is little to distinguish between entrances to businesses and entrances to residential cores. There are significant successes though, including the nursery's play-space, which animates one of the courtyards as well as a popular 'destination' café, and an interesting cross-section of businesses housed in the distinctive and variable-sized units.

COMMENTARY

Despite the laudable effort and determination that has gone into achieving this impressive and immensely complex three-dimensional configuration of living, working and socialising, the limited scope it offers for replicability – in terms of both cost and practicality – means that we are unlikely to see 8 Houses springing up across the world. Its relevance lies rather in its reimagining of deck-access housing, which has been largely abandoned in the UK due to its associations with failed modernist social housing schemes such as at Park Hill in Sheffield (see Chapter 1), and in its incorporation of supporting community and business uses. There are also some lessons to be learned in terms of the demarcation of boundaries, which are eroded at many levels in the ambiguous territory of the ramped street and perhaps overly subtle demarcation of 'private' areas, but most notably in the overall visible intensity of the scheme, which presents a ten-storey wall of 'eyes' from the inner balconies of many dwellings.

This is nevertheless an interesting and important case study, setting a whole new standard for innovation in mixed-use housing schemes that challenges our presumptions about deck-access housing, combining visionary with customary traditional and contemporary typologies. The ambitious unravelling, merging and tinkering of standard approaches to circulation and the renegotiation of assumed public/private thresholds creates a distinctive and extraordinary place and a timely reminder of the potential deck-access design solutions offer to combine sustainable densities with a social agenda.

Successes

- Figure-of-eight form breaks what would otherwise be one large courtyard into two smaller ones and enlivens the street façades with indents and inlets.
- Crossover point allows access to both courtyards and creates a natural focus for lifts and stair cores.
- Highly responsive to views and context, rising dramatically from south to north, so allowing sunlight to penetrate deep into the block's interior, while maximising views out to the nature reserve from apartments.
- Reimagines modernist deck access to dwellings in the form of an innovative spiral ramped circulation route ascending the interior of the block, imbuing the scheme with a social 'heart'.

Drawbacks

- Tension between the semi-public use of the deck and the occupiers of the individual private gardens.
- Three-dimensional form is complex and expensive to design and build.

4.20 Interior images of 8 House: (top) 'streets in the sky'; (bottom) front gardens extending off the ramped street.

'SUBURBAN' CASE EXAMPLES

POUNDBURY, DORSET, UK

Reliving times past

Location: *Dorset, UK*
Date of completion: *Construction began in 1993, 50% complete in 2010, ongoing to 2022*
Urban context: *Urban extension*
Client: *Duchy of Cornwall*
Masterplanners: *Léon Krier and Alan Baxter Associates*
Area: *LHS 0.46 hectares / RHS 0.42 hectares*
Block dimensions: *LHS 84 × 81m / RHS 102 × 62m (largest measurements)*
Number of dwellings: *LHS 25 / RHS 26*
Land use: *Housing*
Tenure: *Mixed*
Parking: *Mews courtyard*

PROJECT ORIGINS
Poundbury is essentially a 'new town' initiated by the Prince of Wales on land owned by the Duchy of Cornwall in Dorset, near Dorchester. Construction began in 1993, and it has been criticised for its historicist architecture and nostalgic overtones. Its royal patronage also makes it a highly unusual case, yet it is one so redolent of Britain's own 'New Urbanist' movement, and so influential on subsequent suburban development, that it is worth revisiting from the point of view of its urban form and block structure.

The first phase of development followed New Urbanist principles: traditional building forms focused on a walkable network of streets and squares, and referenced the local architectural vernacular. It also sought to emulate some of the loftier principles of the Garden City Movement, by incorporating mixed-uses and employment opportunities, in the hope it would develop into a more or less self-sustained settlement, rather than a mere dormitory for commuters.

BLOCK CONFIGURATION
Figure 4.21 shows two irregularly shaped blocks (labelled LHS and RHS in key info above) forming part of the first phase of development. The two blocks are separated by a shared-surface street running north to south that restricts car access to its extremities, and is the reason we are reading it as a 'block of two halves'. They can be read either as a pair or as a unit,

in the sense that the complexity of the layout – incorporating routes through and between the block(s) – blurs boundaries between what is public at one end of the spectrum, and what is private at the other.

The plan illustrates the principles adopted for many of the Poundbury urban blocks: a clearly defined perimeter of houses with a more or less continuous building line enclosing a looser interior court, which is also overlooked by fronts as well as backs of dwellings. The perimeter of the block is broken to allow cars into it, but the overall effect, at least as seen from the outside, is of a traditional street made up of row housing (see Figure 4.23). Most of the houses are two storeys in height, with three-storey units marking prominent corners. In the illustrated example, the corners 'step out' over the footpath, further emphasising the symbolic importance accorded to block corners in contemporary urban design practice.

Both blocks show an innovative feature referred to as 'chequerboarding', whereby some of the house plots are reversed so that the front of the house overlooks the parking area, rather than the street (see Figure 4.24). So-called 'coach house' typologies are also liberally deployed within the courts. These are a common building type in Britain, incorporating flats over garages ('FOGs' in less esteemed company). The majority of blocks provide for more than one pedestrian route through, fostering the sense of a connected network of streets, alleys and courtyards.

COMMENTARY
The irregular block planning of Poundbury's first phase of development demonstrates that the perimeter block typology need not be synonymous with gridded layouts, so much so that it has been described as 'relentlessly informal'.[7] In this sense, it can be described as a kind of 'planned organicism', because the impression of organic growth belies the fixity of the masterplan that underlies it.

Behind the scenes the mixing of tenures and house types shows a genuine concern to create mixed communities and neighbourhoods. Arising from its removal of cars from the street, however, access to many of the houses is also from the back. In many respects this is the Achilles heel of Poundbury's block structure, because it has created street fronts that feel eerily deserted instead of being the lively traditional streets it

4.21 Block plan of Poundbury.

0   25   50m

4.22 Aerial view of Poundbury.

sought to emulate. In so doing, it has arguably designed the block around the car, rather than around the pedestrian as was originally intended.

The predominance of row housing combined with flats over garages drives the density of dwellings per hectare significantly higher than most suburban schemes in the UK. Research indicates that this density crosses the threshold whereby sustainable and walkable neighbourhoods are more likely to succeed, because they pack enough people into the catchment within which most people are prepared to walk to them, rather than drive. This itself is of interest because house prices at Poundbury are consistently higher than comparable developments in the surrounding area,[8] and shows that higher densities can be successful.

Development at Poundbury is ongoing and scheduled for completion in 2022. The Prince's Foundation is currently developing schemes based on similar principles at Tregunnel Hill and the outskirts of Newquay at Nansledan in Cornwall, but its influence is evidenced most often on schemes that are decidedly suburban in terms of their context and character, with much lower densities and a greater preponderance of detached and semi-detached house types, which ironically are indicative of the sorts of development Prince Charles railed against to begin with.

Successes
- The irregular form of the block with minimal or no set-backs creates a varied and attractive streetscape that is well overlooked and has a strong sense of enclosure.
- Wide range of house types successfully addresses corners and allows the built frontage to change direction at different angles.
- High degree of pedestrian permeability through its inhabited core.

Drawbacks
- Car parking is relegated to the inside of the block, thereby reducing the frequency of use of front doors, and diluting the success of the street as a place.

4.23 Street view of Poundbury.

4.24 'Chequerboarding at Poundbury', with some houses oriented to overlook the interior parking court instead of the street.

KINGS HILL

Planned picturesque

Location: *West Malling, Kent, UK*
Date of completion: *2006 (ongoing)*
Urban context: *New town*
Client: *Liberty Property Trust UK*
Masterplanners: *Clague Architects / BDB*
Area: *0.79 hectares*
Block dimensions: *115m × 84m (largest measurements)*
Number of dwellings: *27*
Land use: *Housing*
Tenure: *Mixed*
Parking: *Mixed (on-plot garage, on-plot car barns)*[9]

PROJECT ORIGINS

Kings Hill is the site of a former Royal Air Force base that was used intensively during World War II before being purchased from the Ministry of Defence by Kent County Council. The Council selected it for the construction of one of several new settlements. The original intention was to develop the site for employment uses, but the decision was taken to 'add on' some residential development in 1994, with a view to making the provision of local services benefitting the employment uses more viable. As time passed, however, the balance of uses shifted inexorably towards residential use, of a scale requiring a full range of local services – schools, shops, sports and medical facilities, etc. – to support the burgeoning new village-cum-town.

The approach to masterplanning can be read as the product of several different strands of traditional and contemporary urban design (townscape, garden city, walkable neighbourhoods, defensible space, etc.) tempered by commercial expedience.

The overall urban structure of the place is organised around a central spine route (conceived as an avenue) that joins each phase to the next. Along this route there is a sequence of urban design 'set pieces', taking the form of circuses or crescents and culminating in the apotheosis of English rural idyll – a cricket pitch – with further informal residential courtyards and closes branching off it. The avenue itself is (in comparison to many UK schemes) generously paved in red concrete block pavers with grey granite-coloured detailing rather than the ubiquitous tarmac found in many contemporaneous projects, while generous landscaped verges further enhance the character and greenery of the scheme.

The seemingly organic nature of the street network, means that legibility is arguably limited without access to mapping and it's easy to lose one's way or to find onself down a dead-end street. This is a noteworthy feature because while the masterplan is generally permeable and has deliberately avoided creating a dendritic series of cul-de-sacs, its complexity means that navigability is challenging in terms of both direction and its public/private boundaries. Cul-de-sacs have instead been replaced by a combination of private drives and mews courts that are more or less permeable to pedestrians, but are designed and signed to send a clear message to people using them – that they have crossed a threshold separating the public realm from the rather more ambiguous semi-private realm.

BLOCK CONFIGURATION

The illustrated block (see Figure 4.25) is irregular in shape with somewhat ambiguous extents. While its southern extremity is clearly defined by the above-mentioned avenue (from which the block is accessed), on departing from the avenue there is a subtle transition to private drive and pedestrian pathway via a shared-surface street, which itself gives access to a series of parking courts that are partially inhabited either by flats over garages or houses. Some of these provide rear parking and service access to a frontage of houses facing onto the cricket pitch (see Figure 4.26).

Compared to traditional gridded masterplans where each block is defined by a street, the blocks at Kings Hill are less clearly distinguished from one another. The extent to which Figure 4.25 is coloured reflects the degree to which, it could be argued, the block is identifiable as a coherent entity, but other interpretations are possible. The point here is that the combination of interwoven forms is both sophisticated and ambiguous, but not problematically so. In terms of the block's inward- and outward-facing qualities, the configuration works hard to address both simultaneously which has imbued the scheme with a charmingly jumbled character though also necessitated some compromises in clarity. The effective interweaving of fronts and backs does, however, prevent the creation of any spaces that are definitively 'back-of-house' and the antisocial activity these attract, while also generating a spatially intriguing network for pedestrians (see Figure 4.28).

4.25 Block plan of Kings Hill.

0   25   50m

4.26 Aerial view of Kings Hill.

4.27 Exterior images of Kings Hill: (top) a quintessentially English cricket pitch marks the centre of the neighbourhood; (bottom) pedestrian routes between blocks.

4.28 Interior images of Kings Hill: (top) set-back house within parking court beyond; (bottom) view within parking court.

COMMENTARY

The development as a whole is an in-direct homage to the Garden City Movement, without the original Garden City Movement's underlying commitment to achieving social justice. Its form (including the illustrated block) fits the description of 'planned picturesque' and in this regard can be seen as a continuation of Britain's own New Urbanist legacy in the manner of Poundbury. In contrast to Poundbury, there is a sense that the house types have been minimally adapted from standard plans rather than being designed to fit the masterplan or the place as such. The overall mix is of generally larger house types wrapped in a 'neo-Kentish meets New England' vernacular and in some areas they appear to have been somewhat shoehorned into the masterplan without prehaps the amount of breathing space they needed to sit comfortably next to each other. Nevertheless, its location within striking distance of London has been cited as underpinning its commercial success, with average house prices significantly above the local average.

As has already been alluded to, the combination of a variety of urban forms – private drive/cul-de-sac, shared-surface street, inhabited and uninhabited parking courts, all within a single block – gives the overall impression of a place that, depending on one's point of view, either lacks a clear urban structure, and as a result is difficult to navigate, or is richly layered, and doesn't need one. While the block structure could be criticised for its lack of clarity and some other aspects,[10] there are many UK suburbs that exhibit much clearer block structure yet are far less attractive. Clearly there are other factors at work, and it is suggested that the flexibility afforded by combining urban forms has allowed the 'picturesque' aspects of the scheme to be manifested in ways that would be difficult to achieve with a more structured approach.

Successes

- The richly layered network generates a unique sense of place with a picturesque aesthetic.
- The engineered geometry of the access roads is suburban in character; however, this is offset by judicious deployment of a range of surface treatments (including shared surfaces), thus avoiding the sense of monotony associated with tarmac.
- The size allows for a reasonable degree of permeability around the block.
- A range of on-plot and off-plot parking solutions is used to minimise the intrusion of parked cars, including flats over garages, parking courts, parking barns and garages.

Drawbacks

- Restricted palette of standardised house types within an organic urban plan means that they do not all sit easily with the shape of the block, especially at its corners.
- While the entry point to the interior of the block is well overlooked, the inner courts are constrained by the depth of the units and larger back gardens.

ABODE AT GREAT KNEIGHTON

Contextualising the suburban block

Location: *Trumpington, South Cambridge, UK*
Date of completion: *2014*
Urban context: *Urban extension*
Client: *Countryside Properties*
Masterplanners: *Proctor and Matthews Architects*
Area: *0.26 hectares*
Block dimensions: *47m × 49m (largest dimension)*
Number of dwellings: *9*
Land use: *Housing*
Tenure: *Mixed*
Parking: *On-street and on-plot*

PROJECT ORIGINS

Abode at Great Kneighton is part of a larger development planned to accommodate around 2250 new homes on the southern fringe of Cambridge. The developer, Countryside Properties, is a volume UK house-builder which, unusually for the UK market, has a strong track record of supporting contemporary design and innovative approaches to masterplanning.[11] The development as a whole also provides for schools, a country park, children's play, local services and (in partnership with Liberty Property Trust), a biomedical campus.

The block plan (Figure 4.29) sits at the edge of a larger scheme designed by Proctor and Matthews Architects that transitions in scale and formality from a large formal courtyard (enclosed by apartment blocks and referencing the traditional Cambridge colleges) through traditional mews blocks (comprised of row housing), and finally the subject blocks, comprised of detached and semi-detached houses (with one row of three row houses) arranged along a sequence of shared-surface 'lanes'. The architect's stated intention is to create 'a relaxed urban erosion' at the edge of the development that contrasts with the stronger urban forms of the courtyard and mews blocks, providing a link through to the countryside beyond.[12] This vision is clearly illustrated in their 'extended' aerial concept sketch (see Figure 4.30), although some key aspects have altered since this was drawn, most notably the orientation of the rows of mews houses.

BLOCK CONFIGURATION

The main blocks are made up of small numbers (six to nine) of houses defined by two streets running in an east–west direction which are crossed by a sequence of shared-surface 'lanes' running north–south towards a small area of woodland to the north of the site. The houses themselves are oriented at 90 degrees to the east–west streets so that most of them face onto the lanes. The streets themselves are informal in character, with build-outs creating pinch points combined with raised tables to help slow traffic. The overall pattern is interrupted by one apartment block located towards the south-eastern corner. The mews blocks to the south are made up of row houses 'bookended' by detached units at each end which act as a kind of 'gateway' or precursor to the looser urban structure that follows (see Figure 4.31).

Parking is provided along both the shared-surface lanes and main streets, with some parking 'on-plot'.

The architects characterise the lanes separating the house fronts as 'landscaped ribbons', and at first glance, it is tempting to mistake the overall urban form as a 'ribbon block'. Closer inspection reveals that the orientation of the built forms in the same direction disguises the fact that they do, in fact, form a combination of two-sided blocks (similar in form to traditional housing blocks) with some perimeter blocks, whereby the houses at the short ends of one block have been planned internally so that their form follows the pattern set by the houses fronting the long sides of the block. Thus, each side of the block is 'fronted' by a house, and so meets the definition of a perimeter block, albeit rather loosely configured.

The linear forms of the houses, combined with gabled fronts and the use of black boarding, references the local vernacular 'long houses' found in many Cambridgeshire villages.[13] In contrast to many examples of ribbon block forms, the north–south 'lanes' are staggered and the east–west streets have been slightly cranked in places so that some houses act as a 'visual stop', holding the view as one approaches. Together, these devices avoid creating a monotonous feel to the scheme usually associated with open-ended ribbon forms and goes a long way towards achieving the 'village atmosphere' intended by the designers (see Figure 4.32).

DIF FEELING
WALKING
EAST-WEST
(MORE URBAN)
VS SOUTH-NORTH
(MORE SUB-
MORE RELAXED?)

4.29 Block plan of Abode.

0   25   50m

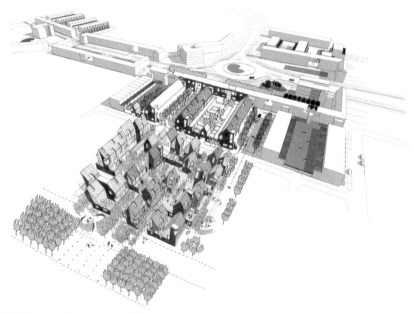

4.30 Extended aerial view of Abode concept scheme.

COMMENTARY

The received wisdom would have it that row blocks (i.e. with frontage to the long side of the block and flank walls or gables to the short sides) are a second-rate form because the ends of the block tend not to be overlooked. Where the gable ends of houses are solid, they can also act as a blank canvas for would-be graffiti artists. In this case the house gables are punctuated by numerous window openings as well as corner windows, and so the criticism does not hold in the same way as it does to many Victorian-era row blocks.

The scheme has received many plaudits and, bearing in mind it departs from the received orthodoxy of block planning in several respects, the high quality of design and landscaping has been combined with a thoughtful and fresh approach to the masterplan to produce a pleasant environment.

Successes

- Small blocks facilitate a high degree of pedestrian permeability.
- Narrow width of the block is achieved by deployment of wide-fronted dwellings with relatively shallow back gardens and reduced back-to-back separation distances.
- Gable ends are carefully designed to address both the street and block corners.
- Averts associations with more standard 'suburban' estates through unusual visual devices and features, such as build-outs, pinch points and minimal turning radii.

Drawbacks

- The modest block size sacrifices garden depth.
- The reduced separation distances may compromise privacy between dwellings.
- The loose arrangement with predominantly wide-fronted house types is not very space efficient, however the reduced garden depths compensate for this to some degree.

4.31 Exterior views of Abode: (top) 'landscaped ribbon' between mews houses and black timber dwellings; (bottom) bookend corner house marks the transition between higher density mews and lower density study block.

4.32 Interior views of Abode: (top) 'shared space' between house fronts within block; (bottom) circular access road to northern edge of block.

'PERI-URBAN' CASE EXAMPLES

COURT HOUSING

A stylish quartet of red-hued gables

Location: *Cortinghborg, Groningen, the Netherlands*
Date of completion: *2013*
Urban context: *Suburban extension*
Client: *Public (local municipality with housing association)*
Architect: *architecten|en|en*
Area: *0.27 hectares*
Block dimensions: *56m × 48m (largest measurements)*
Number of dwellings: *96 townhouses in four blocks of 24 dwellings each*
Land use: *Housing*
Tenure: *Social rent*
Parking: *Car-free project with limited on-street parking*

PROJECT ORIGINS

This housing development is located on a former sports field within the northern ring road of the Dutch town of Groningen. In 2010 the city authorities launched a project called 'Bouwjong' (which translates as 'Build Young') to provide affordable housing for young people in a bid to not only attract students to the city, but to keep them after they graduate, by offering attractive starter homes.

The Bouwjong project designated four zones in the city where 4500 'youth housing' units could be developed. One of these zones for youth housing is Cortinghborg, where architecten|en|en's Court Housing is located. Court Housing is one segment of a tripartite development of three schemes by different architects. Directly to the north is an apartment scheme by Diederendirrix architects, taking the form of a dramatic 400m linear wall of accommodation along the edge of the ring road to the north and acting as a sound barrier for the lower-rise Court Housing to the south. A 70m high round tower designed by De Unie Architecten, of 220 units, also sits on the east end of the site and combines student accommodation with apartments. The Court Housing element is much lower density than its neighbours and provides amply proportioned homes with gardens, attractive to young families, thus aligning with project Bouwjong's objectives to offer incentives for the student population to settle in the city on a longer-term basis.

BLOCK CONFIGURATION

The blocks lie directly north of a well-regarded and successful post-war housing development 'De Oude Hoogte' (translated as 'garden village'), and the width of the perimeter blocks for Court Housing was determined by extending the existing street network of De Hoogte in a northerly direction. In this way the project continues as a natural extension of De Hoogte, yet it differs significantly in its urban configuration (see Figure 4.33). The Court Housing blocks are truncated to approximately one-third of the length of the elongated De Hoogte development of more traditional row housing, thus greatly increasing the permeability of the new zone. Meanwhile, the skewing of the block geometry creates unusual funnel-shaped streets that open up towards the wall of apartments to the north, thereby generating a shared amenity space that links the developments together. These trapezoid-shaped streets benefit from well-considered lawns and planting located to maximise their solar gain, yet this open space – akin to the shared lozenge-shaped gardens set within the De Hoogte development – is achieved at the expense of continuing the proportional containment of the street structure (see Figure 4.34). In this respect, the scheme configuration also veers away from the advantages of the simple tenure-ship model that row housing traditionally offers, by generating shared landscaped amenity space that requires some form of shared management and funding arrangement. Moreover, the shared amenity space is provided in-between the blocks (rather than within each block enclosure) so is effectively shared by the accommodation lining each side of the street rather than each block.

The scheme, typified by its angular roofs and stylistic colour hues, is comprised of four blocks sitting side by side, each providing 24 terraced houses and 96 residences in total. The accommodation is primarily housing, although the corner units offer scope for occupation as live/work units. The project doesn't include parking within the blocks; instead there is provision for parallel parking on the surrounding streets, where the visual presence of vehicles is minimised by the generous extent of green landscape provided around them. The urban blocks themselves are relatively small in scale, each measuring 65m × 45m, while the row house plots are approx. 5.1m wide by 9.9m long, allowing a certain generosity of proportion to these double-aspect terraced dwellings. The block forms are ostensibly 'row blocks' in type, although these have been reconceptualised into perimeter block form. The design works hard to successfully address many of the accepted pitfalls of

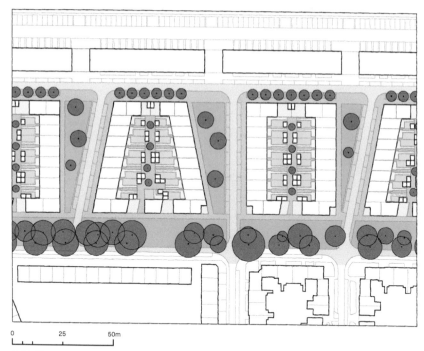

4.33 Block plan of Court Housing.

0   25   50m

4.34 Aerial view of Court Housing.

this most rudimentary block type, and much can be learned from the approach taken here.

Externally, the scheme strongly reflects the local vernacular in terms of its scale, detailing and some of its edge conditions, although with a distinctly contemporary vibe (see Figure 4.35). While the adjacent De Hoogte housing, which these contemporary blocks loosely reflect, offers low-level shrubbery and a 1m set-back from the pavement, the Court Housing blocks meet the street in a much bolder way, with large door-scale windows located directly on the street edge and no transition zone offering privacy (see Figure 4.35). This works better in situations where the façades open onto shared amenity space but is perhaps more problematic on the façades that directly abut the roadways, where blinds are more likely to be drawn. The 'special' corners, meanwhile, cut away the volume at ground and first floors to provide outer corner units with undercroft gardens (see Figure 4.35). These are surrounded by a fine mesh fencing, offering a tantalising glimpse of the occupation within while largely retaining residents' privacy. These eye-catching, white rendered corner cutaways reference the local vernacular but also play an excellent role in turning the blocks inside out, artfully enlivening the streetscape.

Another key aspect of the design is the treatment of what would have been considered the 'side streets' of a row housing type, usually edged by the blank gabled sides of the houses. At Court Housing, 'special' dwellings have been designed to address this blank gable condition, which effectively turn the two-directional row housing type into a four-directional perimeter block, offering entrances and windows to living spaces onto the ends of the blocks. The volumetric nature of the 'specials' also visually ties together what would be two independent rows into one entity, by maintaining some full-height façades on each side of the block, all linked by a continuous roof structure. This lends the scheme a pure, almost Roman courtyard block roofscape when viewed from above, imparting little evidence of a hierarchical nature to the two sides of the block. These 'specials' also go a little further than addressing simply the corners and are also used to provide one-off residences in the middle of the widest ends of the blocks. The care and design attention given to achieve a visually continuous façade treatment around all four sides of the block is impressive and effective, with strong potential for replication.

These reconceptualised 'row' blocks are based on traditional Dutch row housing, which offers a shared rear amenity

4.35 Exterior views of Court Housing: (top) angled street connection to De Hoogte, (bottom) access to shared rear access route.

4.36 Interior views of Court Housing: (top) a glimpse of the contrasting walls to the inner court; (bottom) the expanded inner access route.

The development process for this large-scale and ambitious project was unlocked by the municipality agreeing to underwrite significant loans to property developers and housing corporations on the basis that they would agree to work together. The plans for the zones were then developed using a participatory process involving community consultation, during which public exhibitions of the proposals were displayed, and an associated book was even published in collaboration with Delft University of Technology. The whole zone is under the management of a local housing association (De Huismeesters Groningen), providing affordable homes for rent rather than ownership. Court Housing therefore emerges from a specific set of circumstances that firstly promoted targeting of a specific age segment of society, and secondly, benefitted from the support of the local authority in its financing and in pushing an agenda of quality through collaboration. Such a configuration is achievable when a development has an overarching landlord (the housing association in this case) but provision of this generous and un-demarcated landscape – with associated financial overheads – has management maintenance implications that require careful consideration.

passageway with externally accessed storage units/sheds. In this case, however, the typology is modified to expand the scale of these access routes, transforming them into more generous shared courtyard spaces (see Figure 4.36). This subtle move alters the balance of public and private outdoor space within the block enclosure, in recognition of the informal interactions and community bonds that often occur within such amenity spaces. This shared space is effectively 'borrowed' from the rear gardens of residents, a move which aligns with the objectives of such a housing association client, whose priority of establishing a strong sense of community is high in comparison to the retail value associated with every square metre of the rear garden provision. In addition to this expansion of the rear passages, the storage units accessed from rear amenity passages are also enlarged in some instances and provided with windows so as to become occupiable as garden rooms. These extended dwelling spaces – directly overlooking the rear passageway – shift what is traditionally a simple access route into a kind of semi-private street, with informal overlooking imparting the consequent benefits of defensible space.

Court Housing is most interesting for the way it successfully addresses some of the downsides associated with row blocks. In its skilful turning of corners, visual strength as a block form, adoption of small scale blocks, subtle referencing of the vernacular, and expanded amenity areas, Court Housing offers many useful lessons in block design that could be applied elsewhere.

Successes

- The block successfully addresses each side of the street.
- The block size is relatively small, allowing a high degree of permeability.
- Single-entry service lane in the centre of the block(s) is gated and doesn't raise the same security issues as with open-ended service lanes in traditional row blocks.

Drawbacks

- Parking is pushed to the public street, which can be a drawback for residents.
- The block does not incorporate any set-back from the pavement, and the extent of curtaining visible reflects this.

NEPTUNE LOGEMENTS

Relaxed regeneration with a pinch of sea salt

Location: *Grand Large District, Dunkerque, France*
Date of completion: *2012*
Urban context: *Peri-urban renewal*
Client: *Partnership of public authority, private developer and housing association*
Architects: *RSHP (concept masterplanners) and ANMA (masterplanners and project architects)*
Area: *0.46 hectares*
Block dimensions: *62m × 74m (largest measurements)*
Number of dwellings: *81 apartments*
Land use: *Housing*
Tenure: *Mixed social rent and intermediate rent, and ownership*
Parking: *Limited on-street residents' parking with integral garages*

PROJECT ORIGINS

This project is a peri-urban exercise in industrial regeneration striving for block-based diversity. The so-called 'Neptune Project' – centred on the former Dunkerque shipyards – was initiated by municipal authorities in 1991 to address swathes of abandoned land to the north of the city centre following the demise of the shipyards a decade earlier. The brief aimed to turn the city to face the waterfront and was progressive in terms of its ambitions for diversification, combining private and rented housing with community amenities into a dense and cultural new 'peri-urban' neighbourhood. The masterplan was commissioned with phased provision for 23 building and landscape projects to be undertaken by a team of local architects, landscape architects and artists.

'Grand Large District' is the second phase of the Neptune renewal project. The 216 dwellings completed in the whole Neptune phase effectively achieve 'blind tenure', without any apparent distinction between different types of ownership or occupation. The complete (and as yet unfinished) ANMA masterplan will eventually include over 1000 homes.

BLOCK CONFIGURATION

The blocks are comprised of four hybrid perimeter/courtyard blocks arranged in a row, as a set piece (see Figure 4.37).

The waterfront edge itself – the 'front' of the four blocks – is composed of apartments facing south-west over the docks, arranged into what appear on first glance to be a series of 12 *grandes maisons*, each clad dramatically in reflective silver with tall gabled fronts, and a narrow zone of set-back façade between each (see Figure 4.39). These *maisons* vary in height between five and six storeys, with the uppermost storeys squeezed into the narrowing slope of the eaves, and are referred to by the architects as 'The Gables'. The regular rhythm of the recessed links between these 12 'gables' lends the waterfront façade an elegant vertical proportionality, while also serving to minimise the visual impact of the two complete breaks between blocks where minor access streets occur. The architect describes how the relatively tall mass of 'gabled' accommodation to the south-west provides a wind barrier between the docks and the courtyard areas behind, which are semi-enclosed by lower three-storey accommodation embodying a very different visual character of timber and brick.[14]

The specific block illustrated is the largest of the four, with a length of 74m and a depth of 61m. The block (and its immediate neighbours) is comprised entirely of apartments and operates as a hybrid of both courtyard and perimeter block forms, given its offer of entrances from both outside and within the blocks. The simple rectangular block is visibly demarcated by the shape of its perimeter accommodation, yet remains highly permeable to pedestrians with four full-height access points separating the physical massing of apartments, and free-flowing open access to the internal courtyard areas within (see Figure 4.40), where loosely planned stepping-stone routes are laid out along presumed desire lines. This low-level broken massing combined with the resident-occupied and planted inner courts, lends the whole scheme an egalitarian, friendly and welcoming interior. Its soft centre, however, contrasts somewhat with the exterior sides and (to a lesser extent) rear of the blocks, which are dominated by garage doors at ground level. This dead frontage presented by the garage fronts, is moderated to some extent by the dual-aspect nature of the accommodation, which combined with entrances to vertical circulation cores, helps to prevent the back side of the block from entirely turning its back on the street.

The configuration adopts another unusual feature in that the row of taller waterfront 'gable' accommodation is separated from the inner courtyard it shares with the lower-rise

4.37 Block plan of Neptune.

0   25   50m

4.38 Aerial view of Neptune.

4.39 Exterior views of Neptune (front façade of block showing 'The Gables').

apartments, by a narrow through service route. This access road allows for some residents' parking, both parallel, and head-on facing into the shared courtyard on a shared surface. This divided block configuration creates an inner court of two halves, and in this sense sets up a hybrid form of block in which the separated low-rise accommodation that defines the three sides of the courtyard garden becomes almost reminiscent of the 'close' that we have seen in traditional garden suburb designs. Such a configuration might be criticised for being naturally divisive, defining a hierarchy of communities, however at Neptune, the tall waterfront rows and the rear timber courtyard rows both include a mix of tenures – an achievement of the diversity prerogative that was enabled by the multi-headed client.

COMMENTARY

The progressive approach to regeneration and masterplanning underpinning the Neptune Project, means this block is situated on a network that is unusually pedestrian-friendly, which has a significant impact on the arrangement of forms. The perimeter of the block here is very loose, with a relaxed circulation arrangement and relatively free flow of movement into and across the inner courts. The inner and outer characters of the block become merged in this context, and both courtyard and street façades are difficult to distinguish, presenting a similar outlook and accessibility. The relationship between the dwellings and courtyards is similarly relaxed, and homes are designed with the expectation that life will spill out into communal areas. The casual yet carefully executed approach to demarcation of territory, combined with well-considered sightlines and circulation, sets the scene for a lively and contented community to establish itself here. The filtering of traffic allows this informal configuration, but as an ambition of healthy urbanism that best practice is striving for, this almost car-free project could offer plenty of lessons for the design of similar blocks in the future.

Successes

- The linear bars of accommodation leave the inner courtyard open and permeable to the street network, achieving a good balance between efficiency and permeability.
- Surface parking provided inside the block is thoughtfully integrated into the landscaping so it does not dominate.
- Tenure blind.

Drawbacks

- Parking for the courtyard units is primarily in integral garages, creating some lengths of 'dead' frontage.
- The street side of the block that fronts onto the main access road lacks a defensible set-back space and residents have responded accordingly with heavy blinds and security shutters that have a negative impact on the quality of the street.
- The ends of the blocks do not turn corners or address the way into the courtyard in a meaningful way, and adjacent spaces are consequently vulnerable to misuse.

4.40 Interior views of Neptune: (top) interior courtyard of block; (bottom) pedestrian route winding through blocks.

STEIGEREILAND

Plot-based block design

Location: *Ijburg, Amsterdam, the Netherlands*
Date of completion: *1997 (ongoing)*
Urban context: *Peri-urban*
Client: *Multiple private clients*
Architect: *Multiple*
Area: *0.79 hectares*
Block dimensions: *104m × 80m (largest measurements)*
Number of plots: *16 mews and 32 townhouses/apartments*
Land use: *Housing*
Tenure: *Mixed*
Parking: *Carports (mews) and street*

PROJECT ORIGINS

The block is located on Steigereiland, one of six man-made islands collectively known as Ijburg, sitting in Amsterdam's eastern harbour. The project was identified as a VINEX location (a new development area identified by the Dutch Ministry of Housing, Spatial Planning and Environment) in the late 1980s (originally named 'New East' or Nieuw-Oost) and was given the go-ahead by the municipality in 1996, with Steigereiland and Haveneiland comprising the first phase of development.

The advance provision of infrastructure in Ijburg has been likened to the rolling out of a 'red carpet', where a publicly owned, dedicated delivery organisation (Project Bureau Ijburg) acted to continuously mediate between all of the utility and infrastructure providers. To facilitate close grain plot-based development, the municipality – the City of Amsterdam (DRO) – not only reclaimed the land itself but took this one step further. By preparing its own masterplan (in collaboration with local architects), acting as the land developer and funding the infrastructure upfront, it retained tight control of the design method and delivery, to the extent of preparing its own design code, and even appointing a 'block coach' to coordinate the input of individual architects working in a local area.

The development method involved setting out and constructing the piled foundations for individual plots, thereby removing the logistical difficulties of different builders having to operate side by side. These 'serviced plots' were then sold to developers who had to comply with the DRO design code. The municipality reduced its exposure to risk by entering a public–private partnership whereby it pledged to provide the land and most of the infrastructure, and in return agreed to sell the land at a pre-agreed price.

BLOCK CONFIGURATION

The illustrated block is configured as a simple rectangular 'mews block' (see Figures 4.41 and 4.42), with three- and four-storey townhouses/duplexes facing the main east–west streets, small-scale apartment buildings niftily turning the corners, and a secondary mews lane serving a subsidiary frontage of mainly two-storey detached dwellings. Traditional mews blocks, with their main frontages facing the long sides of the block, usually expose blank flank walls to the short sides. Here the apartment buildings on each corner include generous fenestration to the short sides of the block, while the end mews houses that edge these side streets have their main entrances located on this side (see Figure 4.43). The turning of corners and location of entrances were factors stipulated in the overarching design code, and the outcome clearly illustrates how the benefits of both control and freedom can add up to something greater than the sum of its parts.

The block is an interesting inversion of hierarchical mews relationships familiar from the Georgian era, where the larger homes were located on the main streets and 'serviced' by the smaller mews dwellings at the rear, where servants were often accommodated. At Steigereiland, however, the higher value and larger properties are located to the rear, sheltered from the main street, where the mews becomes a secluded 'enclave' as opposed to an access route (see Figure 4.44). Notwithstanding that the contemporary Netherlands is a far less hierarchical kind of society, this does represent a reversed 'social status' from the Georgian origins of the block type. Here the shared surface demarcates a semi-private zone that effectively discourages through traffic, while maintaining pedestrian permeability.

COMMENTARY

Whereas most blocks are undertaken by a single developer, the devolved 'plot-based' approach adopted in Steigereiland and elsewhere across Ijburg cut out the middleman so to speak (i.e. the commercial developer), allowing small-scale developers, individuals and small groups to both design and develop their own plots. In this sense, the block (and others surrounding it) has been developed in the 'traditional' manner,

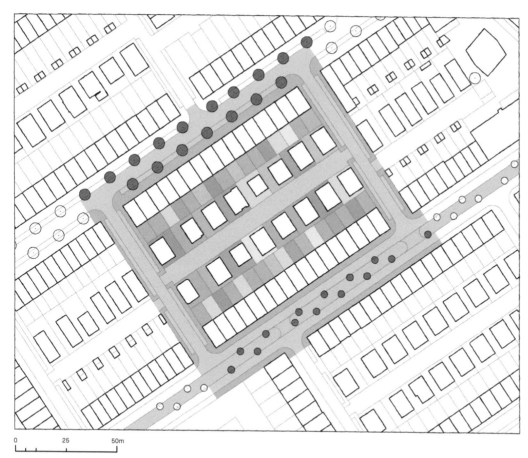

0   25   50m

4.41 Block plan of Steigereiland.

4.42 Aerial view of Steigereiland.

allowing a diversity of designs (and uses) to emerge and, crucially, bestowing a potential for individual plots to change over time in a way 'single project' blocks cannot achieve. Although the individual buildings were required to conform to a design code stipulating overall building parameters, the result is a rich tapestry of unique buildings that still achieves a coherence of form.

Perhaps the biggest challenge to promoting a plot-based approach to masterplanning is that it infers decoupling masterplanning from the design and procurement of the buildings themselves, and allowing a greater range of different designers and developers to contribute. This, in turn, requires an acceptance that placemaking happens over much longer time horizons than individual building projects, and as such, is bigger than any single architect. It involves a culture shift away from the 'starchitect' as omni-influential visionary creator, to accepting the more humble role of facilitator in the first instance and, subsequently, to accepting the role of contributor to the plurality of urban fabric.[15] This kind of 'bottom up' development, as championed by urban designers such as Kelvin Campbell, allows blocks to evolve in a more natural way, and this Ijburg block demonstrates the richness and complexity, as well as the distinctive fine-tuning of space and place that can successfully emerge from such a scenario.

Successes

- The incorporation of a mews lane that is open at both ends and overlooked by dwellings on both sides creates a high degree of permeability and feeling of 'eyes on the street'.
- The combination of townhouses, urban villas and apartments should attract a more balanced community.
- The development of plots (and in some cases small groups of plots) by a range of diverse interests and designed by different architects has resulted in a high degree of design diversity and visual interest, making the block inherently adaptable to change.

Drawbacks

- Tight control over the design code and procurement routes are required to maintain high standards of design overall in this type of plot-based development.
- The quality of design of the individual buildings is variable, highlighting that diversity in some cases can be a weakness.

4.43 Views towards the block corners and external streets at Steigereiland, showing the diversity and grain achieved by the plot-based approach to development.

4.44 View towards interior mews lane.

REFERENCES

INTRODUCTION

1 Kelvin Campbell, *Making Massive Small Change: Building the Urban Society We Want*, White River Junction, VT, USA, Chelsea Green Publishing, 2018, p. 219.

2 Thorsten Bürklin and Michael Pererek, *Urban Building Blocks*, Basel, Birkhäuser, 2008.

3 The UK government's new programme of garden towns being another exception to prove the rule.

4 Department for Communities and Local Government, 'Fixing our Broken Housing Market', February 2017. Available from https://assets.publishing.service.gov.uk/government/uploads/system/uploads/attachment_data/file/590464/Fixing_our_broken_housing_market_-_print_ready_version.pdf (accessed 13 October 2019).

CHAPTER 1

1 Phillippe Panerai, Jean Castex, Jean-Charles Depaule and Ivor Samuels, *Urban Forms: The Death and Life of the Urban Block*, Oxford, Architectural Press, 2004, pp. 158–166.

2 Courtesy Google Earth, Digital Globe, 2019.

3 Charles Gates, *Ancient Cities: The Archaeology of Urban Life in the Ancient Near East and Egypt, Greece and Rome* (second edition), Abingdon, Routledge, 2011.

4 Ibid.

5 Charles Gates, *Ancient Cities: The Archaeology of Urban Life in the Ancient Near East and Egypt, Greece and Rome* (second edition), Abingdon, Routledge, 2011, p. 279.

6 Joseph Rykwert, *The Idea of a Town: An Anthropology of Urban Form in Rome, Italy and the Ancient World*, London, MIT Press, 1988, p. 60.

7 Jeffrey Becker, 'Roman Domestic Architecture: the Insula', 27 February 2016, *Smarthistory*, https://smarthistory.org/roman-domestic-architecture-insula (accessed 13 October 2019).

8 Spiro Kostof, *The City Shaped: Urban Patterns and Meanings Through History*, London, Thames and Hudson, 1991, p. 43.

9 Keith Lilley, 'Urban Planning and the Design of Towns in the Middle Ages: The Earls of Devon and their 'New Towns'', *Planning Perspectives*, 16, 2001, pp. 1–24.

10 Paul Hindle, *Medieval Town Plans*, Princes Risborough, Shire Publications, 1990, p. 51.

11 Spiro Kostof, *The City Shaped: Urban Patterns and Meanings Through History*, London, Thames and Hudson, 1991, p. 45.

12 Ibid, p. 50.

13 Paul Hindle, *Medieval Town Plans*, Princes Risborough, Shire Publications, 1990, p. 51.

14 Canterbury City Council, Canterbury Conservation Area Appraisal, Canterbury, Canterbury City Council, 2012. Available from https://www.canterbury.gov.uk/downloads/file/671/canterbury_conservation_area_appraisal (accessed 13 October 2019).

15 David Rudlin and Nicholas Falk, *Sustainable Urban Neighbourhood: Building the 21st Century Home*, Oxford, Architectural Press, 2009, pp. 62–63.

16 Kelvin Campbell, *Making Massive Small Change: Building the Urban Society We Want*, White River Junction, VT, USA, Chelsea Green Publishing, 2018, p. 121.

17 Spiro Kostof, *The City Shaped: Urban Patterns and Meanings Through History*, London, Thames and Hudson, 1991, p. 96.

18 Eric Firley and Caroline Stahl, *The Urban Housing Handbook*, Chichester, John Wiley and Sons, 2009, pp. 205–209.

19 Eric Firley and Caroline Stahl, *The Urban Housing Handbook*, Chichester, John Wiley and Sons, 2009, p. 245.

20 Yasser Elsheshtawy, 'Urban Dualities in the Arab World: From a Narrative of Loss to Neo-Liberal Urbanism', in M. Larice and E. Macdonald (eds), *The Urban Design Reader* (second edition), New York, Routledge, 2013, p. 477.

21 Coen Beeker, *Woonzekerheid en ruimtelijke herinrichting in Ouagadougou*, Vrije Universiteit Amsterdam, Geografisch en Planologisch Institute, Vakgroep Planologie, https://www.asclibrary.nl/docs/408651938.pdf, 1980 (accessed 13 October 2019).

22 Phillippe Panerai, Jean Castex, Jean-Charles Depaule and Ivor Samuels, *Urban Forms: The Death and Life of the Urban Block*, Oxford, Architectural Press, 2004, p. 40.

23 Michael Larice and Elizabeth MacDonald (eds), *The Urban Design Reader* (second edition), New York, Routledge, 2013, p. 78.

24 Clarence Stein. 'Towards New Town for America' (1957), in B. M. Nicolaides and A. Wiese (eds), *The Suburb Reader*, New York, Routledge, 2006, p. 176.

25 Colin Buchanan, *Traffic in Towns: The Specially Shortened Edition of the Buchanan Report*, Harmondsworth, Penguin Publications Ltd, 1963, p. 57.

26 Ibid, p. 64.

27 Jane Jacobs, *The Death and Life of Great American Cities*, New York, Modern Library, 1961, p. 238.

28 Michael Sorkin, 'The End(s) of Urban Design', in M. Larice and E. Macdonald (eds), *The Urban Design Reader* (second edition), New York, Routledge, 2013, p. 621.

29 Oscar Newman, *Defensible Space: Crime Prevention Through Urban Design*, New York, Macmillan, 1973.

30 Alice M. Coleman, *Utopia on Trial: Vision and Reality in Planned Housing*, London, Hilary Shipman Ltd, 1985.

31 Nicholas Taylor, *The Village in the City: Towards a New Society*, London, Maurice Temple Smith Ltd, 1973.

32 Katharina Borsi, Nicole Porter and Megan Nottingham, 'The Typology of the Berlin Block: History, Continuity and Spatial Performance', *Athens Journal of Architecture*, vol. 2, no. 1, January 2016, pp. 45–64. Available from https://www.athensjournals.gr/architecture/2016-2-1-3-Borsi.pdf (accessed 8 October 2019).

33 Congress for the New Urbanism, Congress for the New Urbanism, 'Charter for the New Urbanism', in M. Larice and E. Macdonald (eds), *The Urban Design Reader* (second edition), New York, Routledge, 2013.

34 Members of the Urban Task Force, *Towards an Urban Renaissance: Final Report of the Urban Task Force*, Department of the Environment, Transport and the Regions, London, E & FN Spon, 1999.

35 English Partnerships and the Housing Corporation, *Urban Design Compendium*, London, English Partnerships, 2000.

CHAPTER 2

1 English Partnerships and the Housing Corporation, *Urban Design Compendium*, London, English Partnerships, 2000, p. 64.

2 Ian Bentley, Alan Alcock, Paul Murrain, Sue McGlynn and Graham Smith, *Responsive Environments: A Manual for Designers*, Oxford, Architectural Press, 1985, p. 14.

3 Ibid.

CHAPTER 3

1 Kelvin Campbell, *Making Massive Small Change: Building the Urban Society We Want*, White River Junction, VT, USA, Chelsea Green Publishing, 2018, pp. 152–153.

2 Ian Bentley, Alan Alcock, Paul Murrain, Sue McGlynn and Graham Smith, *Responsive Environments: A Manual for Designers*, Oxford, Architectural Press, 1985, p. 13.

3 Kelvin Campbell, *Making Massive Small Change: Building the Urban Society We Want*, White River Junction, VT, USA, Chelsea Green Publishing, 2018, p. 115.

4 Kim Dovey, *Urban Design Thinking: A Conceptual Toolkit*, London, Bloomsbury, 2016, p. 18.

5 Members of The Urban Task Force, *Towards an Urban Renaissance: Final Report of the Urban Task Force*, Department of the Environment, Transport and the Regions, London, E & FN Spon, 1999, p. 59.

6 English Partnerships and the Housing Corporation, *Urban Design Compendium*, London, English Partnerships, 2000, p. 38.

7 Kim Dovey, *Urban Design Thinking: A Conceptual Toolkit*, London, Bloomsbury, 2016, p. 19.

8 William Whyte, *The Social Life of Small Urban Spaces*, New York, Project for Public Spaces Inc., 1980.

9 English Partnerships and the Housing Corporation, *Urban Design Compendium*, London, English Partnerships, 2000, p. 88.

10 Jan Gehl, *Life Between Buildings*, London, Island Press, 2011.

11 Jonathan Tarbatt, *The Plot: Designing Diversity in the Built Environment – A Manual for Architects and Urban Designers*, London, RIBA Publishing, 2012, p. 62.

12 Ibid, p. 63.

13 David Levitt, *The Housing Design Handbook: A Guide to Good Practice*, Oxford, Routledge, 2010.

14 Kelvin Campbell, *Making Massive Small Change: Building the Urban Society We Want*, White River Junction, VT, USA, Chelsea Green Publishing, 2018, p. 219.

15 Jonathan Tarbatt, *The Plot: Designing Diversity in the Built Environment – A Manual for Architects and Urban Designers*, London, RIBA Publishing, 2012, p. 12.

16 Ann Sussman and Justin Hollander, *Cognitive Architecture: Designing for How We Respond to the Built Environment*, Abingdon, Routledge, 2015, p. 25.

17 Jan Gehl, *Life Between Buildings*, London, Island Press, 2011, p. 53.

18 CABE, *What Home Buyers Want: Attitudes and Decision Making Among Consumers*, London, Commission for Architecture & the Built Environment, 2005. Available from: https://webarchive.nationalarchives.gov.uk/20110118185910/http://www.cabe.org.uk/files/what-home-buyers-want.pdf (accessed 13 October 2019).

19 David Levitt, *The Housing Design Handbook: A Guide to Good Practice*, Oxford, Routledge, 2010, p. 98.

20 Eric Firley and Caroline Stahl, *The Urban Housing Handbook*, Chichester, John Wiley and Sons, 2009, pp. 107–108.

21 Jan Gehl, *Life Between Buildings*, London, Island Press, 2011, p. 98.

22 Phillippe Panerai, Jean Castex, Jean-Charles Depaule and Ivor Samuels, *Urban Forms: The Death and Life of the Urban Block*, Oxford, Architectural Press, 2004, p. 86.

23 Ann Sussman and Justin Hollander, *Cognitive Architecture: Designing for How We Respond to the Built Environment*, Abingdon, Routledge, 2015, p. 104.

24 Jonathan Tarbatt, *The Plot: Designing Diversity in the Built Environment – A Manual for Architects and Urban Designers*, London, RIBA Publishing, 2012, p. 107.

25 English Partnerships and the Housing Corporation, *Urban Design Compendium*, London, English Partnerships, 2000, p. 88.

26 David Levitt, *The Housing Design Handbook: A Guide to Good Practice*, Oxford, Routledge, 2010.

27 Jonathan Tarbatt, *The Plot: Designing Diversity in the Built Environment – A Manual for Architects and Urban Designers*, London, RIBA Publishing, 2012, p. 140.

CHAPTER 4

1 Hari Phillips, 'Royal Road: Panter Hudspith Architects at Elephant and Castle', *Architecture Today*, vol. 251, September 2014, pp. 28–37. Available from http://media.designersfriend.co.uk/panterhudspith/media/Royal_Road_in_AT_Sep_2014.pdf (accessed 14 October 2019).

2 Bridin O'Connor, Group Manager, DM Strategics Team London Borough of Southwark Planning Department, http://panterhudspith.com/project/royal-road/ (accessed 14 October 2019).

3 Ibid.

4 Ibid.

5 These lost favour in the UK soon after their heyday in the 1960s and 1970s because of their inherent social and practical issues, yet have remained more popular and common in Europe where different management arrangements and social conditions prevail.

6 Kelly Minner, '8 House/BIG', https://www.archdaily.com/83307/8-house-big (accessed 14 October 2019).

7 English Partnerships, *Car Parking: What Works Where*, London, English Partnerships, 2006, p. 124.

8 Graham Norwood, 'Poundbury: A Look at Prince Charles' sustainable village in Dorset, on its 30th birthday', *Daily Telegraph*, 26 April 2017, https://www.telegraph.co.uk/property/buy/poundbury-look-prince-charles-sustainable-village-dorset-30th (accessed 14 October 2019).

9 The term 'car barn' is widely used in the UK to denote a carport or garage structure without a door.

10 For example some of the houses appear to overlook the private gardens of other houses.

11 Countryside Properties has received numerous design awards for contemporary schemes – at Horsted Park, Kent, and Accordia in Cambridge, for example.

12 In this case a block of trees stands in for the countryside, with allotment gardens and older suburban development beyond.

13 Countryside Properties with Proctor and Matthews Architects, 'Abode, Cambridge', Design Council, https://www.designcouncil.org.uk/sites/default/files/asset/document/DC%20CABE%20HOUSING%20CASE%20STUDY_2_ABODE_310316%20FINAL.pdf (accessed 14 October 2019).

14 Nicholas Michelin, 'Grand Large Neptune', ANMA practice self-publication.

15 Jonathan Tarbatt, *The Plot: Designing Diversity in the Built Environment – A Manual for Architects and Urban Designers*, London, RIBA Publishing, 2012, p. 82.

BIBLIOGRAPHY

Becker, J., 'Roman domestic architecture: the insula', 27 February 2016, *Smarthistory*, https://smarthistory.org/roman-domestic-architecture-insula (accessed 13 October 2019).

Beeker, M. C., *Woonzekerheid en ruimtelijke herinrichting in Ouagadougou*, Vrije Universiteit Amsterdam, Geografisch en Planologisch Institute, Vakgroep Planologie, https://www.asclibrary.nl/docs/408651938.pdf, 1980 (accessed 13 October 2019).

Bentley, I. et al., *Responsive Environments: A Manual for Designers*, Oxford, Architectural Press, 1985.

Borsi, K., Porter, N. and Nottingham, M., 'The Typology of the Berlin Block: History, Continuity and Spatial Performance', *Athens Journal of Architecture*, vol. 2, no. 1, January 2016, pp. 45–64. Available from https://www.athensjournals.gr/architecture/2016-2-1-3-Borsi.pdf (accessed 8 October 2019).

Broadbent, G., *Emerging Concepts in Urban Design*, London, E & FN Spon, 1996.

Buchanan, C., *Traffic in Towns: The Specially Shortened Edition of the Buchanan Report*, Harmondsworth, Penguin Publications Ltd, 1963.

Bürklin, T. and M. Pererek, *Urban Building Blocks*, Basel, Birkhäuser, 2008.

CABE, *What Home Buyers Want: Attitudes and Decision Making Among Consumers*, London, Commission for Architecture & the Built Environment, 2005. Available from: https://webarchive.nationalarchives.gov.

uk/20110118185910/http://www.cabe.org.uk/files/what-home-buyers-want.pdf (accessed 13 October 2019).

Campbell, K., *Making Massive Small Change: Building the Urban Society We Want*, White River Junction, VT, USA, Chelsea Green Publishing, 2018.

Canterbury City Council, *Canterbury Conservation Area Appraisal*, Canterbury, Canterbury City Council, 2010. Available from https://www.canterbury.gov.uk/downloads/file/671/canterbury_conservation_area_appraisal (accessed 13 October 2019).

Congress for the New Urbanism, 'Charter for the New Urbanism' (1996), in M. Larice and E. Macdonald (eds), *The Urban Design Reader* (second edition), New York, Routledge, 2013, pp. 328–331.

Cowan, R., *The Dictionary of Urbanism*, Tisbury, Streetwise Press, 2005.

Dovey, K., *Urban Design Thinking: A Conceptual Toolkit*, London, Bloomsbury, 2016.

Elsheshtawy, Y., 'Urban Dualities in the Arab World: From a Narrative of Loss to Neo-Liberal Urbanism' (2011), in M. Larice and E. Macdonald (eds), *The Urban Design Reader* (second edition), New York, Routledge, 2013, pp. 475–496.

English Partnerships, *Car Parking: What Works Where*, London, English Partnerships, 2006.

English Partnerships and the Housing Corporation, *Urban Design Compendium*, London, English Partnerships, 2000.

Firley, E. and C. Stahl, *The Urban Housing Handbook*, Chichester, John Wiley and Sons, 2009.

Gates, C., *Ancient Cities: The Archaeology of Urban Life in the Ancient Near East and Egypt, Greece and Rome* (second edition), Abingdon, Routledge, 2011.

Gehl, J., *Life Between Buildings*, London, Island Press, 2011.

Hindle, P., *Medieval Town Plans*, Princes Risborough, Shire Publications, 1990.

Jacobs, J., *The Death and Life of Great American Cities*, New York, Modern Library, 1961.

Kostof, S., *The City Shaped: Urban Patterns and Meanings Through History*, London, Thames and Hudson, 1991.

Kropf, K., 'Against the Perimeter Block: A Morphological Critique', *Urban Design*, 97, Winter 2006, pp. 12–13.

Larice, M. and E. MacDonald (eds), *The Urban Design Reader* (second edition), New York, Routledge, 2013.

Levitt, D., *The Housing Design Handbook: A Guide to Good Practice*, Oxford, Routledge, 2010.

Lilley, K. D., 'Urban Planning and the Design of Towns in the Middle Ages: The Earls of Devon and their 'New Towns'', *Planning Perspectives*, 16, 2001, pp. 1–24.

Members of The Urban Task Force, *Towards an Urban Renaissance: Final Report of the Urban Task Force*, Department of the Environment, Transport and the Regions, London, E & FN Spon, 1999.

Panerai, P., J. Castex, J.-C. Depaule and I. Samuels, *Urban Forms: The Death and Life of the Urban Block*, Oxford, Architectural Press, 2004.

Rudlin, D. and N. Falk, *Sustainable Urban Neighbourhood: Building the 21st Century Home*, Oxford, Architectural Press, 2009.

Rykwert, J., *The Idea of a Town: An Anthropology of Urban Form in Rome, Italy and the Ancient World*, London, MIT Press, 1988.

Sorkin, M., 'The End(s) of Urban Design' (2006), in M. Larice and E. Macdonald (eds), *The Urban Design Reader* (second edition), New York, Routledge, 2013.

Stein, C., 'Towards New Towns for America' (1957), in B. M. Nicolaides and A. Wiese (eds), *The Suburb Reader*, New York, Routledge, 2006, pp. 176–180.

Sussman, A. and J. Hollander, *Cognitive Architecture: Designing for How we Respond to the Built Environment*, Abingdon, Routledge, 2015.

Tarbatt, J., *The Plot: Designing Diversity in the Built Environment – A Manual for Architects and Urban Designers*, London, RIBA Publishing, 2012.

Tonkiss, F., *Cities by Design*, Cambridge, Polity Press, 2013.

Whyte, W., *The Social Life of Small Urban Spaces*, New York, Project for Public Spaces Inc., 1980.

INDEX

IMAGE CREDITS